FINDING FORGIVENESS IN UNEXPECTED WAYS

BEYOND
THE HURT

HANNA OLIVAS

ALONG WITH 21 INSPIRING AUTHORS

ISBN: 978-1-968061-41-8

TABLE OF CONTENTS

INTRODUCTION

Welcome to *Beyond the Hurt*

Forgiveness. It's a word we hear often, but one that rarely feels simple. For many, it's wrapped in layers of pain, confusion, fear, and—sometimes—hope. In *Beyond the Hurt*, we explore what it truly means to forgive through the voices of women who have walked through the fire and found peace on the other side.

This anthology was born from a shared belief: that stories have the power to heal, connect, and transform. Within these pages, you'll encounter women who have faced betrayal, heartbreak, loss, and disappointment—yet have discovered something unexpected in the process of forgiving: themselves.

Each story is deeply personal, yet universal in its truth. The journeys may differ, but the heartbeat is the same—a desire to let go of pain, reclaim inner peace, and live beyond the hurt.

You won't find perfect endings here. What you will find are honest reflections, hard-won wisdom, and moments of courage that will remind you that you're not alone. Whether you're just beginning to explore forgiveness or are well along your path, these stories are here to walk with you, to offer hope, and to show you that healing is possible—even if it comes in ways you never expected.

So take your time. Sit with these stories. Let them speak to the tender parts of your heart. And as you read, may you begin to see that forgiveness is not weakness—it's strength. It's not forgetting—it's freedom. And it's not the end—it's a new beginning.

Welcome to *Beyond the Hurt*.

Hanna Olivas

Founder and CEO of SHE RISES STUDIOS

https://www.linkedin.com/company/she-rises-studios/
https://www.facebook.com/sherisesstudios
https://www.instagram.com/sherisesstudios_llc/
www.SheRisesStudios.com

Author, Speaker, and Founder. Hanna was born and raised in Las Vegas, Nevada, and has paved her way to becoming one of the most influential women of 2022. Hanna is the co-founder of She Rises Studios and the founder of the Brave & Beautiful Blood Cancer Foundation. Her journey started in 2017 when she was first diagnosed with Multiple Myeloma, an incurable blood cancer. Now more than ever, her focus is to empower other women to become leaders because The Future is Female. She is currently traveling and speaking publicly to women to educate them on entrepreneurship, leadership, and owning the female power within.

Beyond the Hurt: Rising Above Life's Pain and Transforming Tragedy into Triumph

By Hanna Olivas

There's a place deep inside all of us where the echoes of past hurts live. It's where the pain of tragedy, loss, and hardship resides, reminding us of the struggles we've faced. For years, I carried that pain with me like a weight around my heart, unsure of how to move beyond it. But here's what I've learned through my own journey: "Pain does not define you—what you do with it does." And that's what this chapter is about. It's about moving beyond the hurt, about finding the strength within yourself to rise above your past, and about transforming your pain into something powerful, something meaningful, something that drives you forward rather than holds you back.

My Journey Beyond the Hurt

To understand the power of living beyond the hurt, I have to start with my own story. I've faced more pain and heartache than I ever thought possible. I've experienced loss, betrayal, and unimaginable hurt. From my father walking out when I was only eight years old, to losing my son, baby Mario, at eight and a half months pregnant, to being diagnosed with multiple myeloma and breast cancer—all of these experiences left scars on my heart that I wasn't sure I'd ever heal from. But here's what I've come to realize: "The scars we carry are not signs of weakness; they are reminders of our resilience."

There were times when the hurt felt like too much to bear. There were days when I didn't know how to move forward, when the pain seemed to consume everything. But deep down, I knew there had to be more to life than the suffering I was experiencing. I refused to let my pain be the end of my story. And that's when I made a conscious decision to live beyond the hurt.

Living beyond the hurt doesn't mean pretending the pain never happened. It doesn't mean ignoring the scars or forgetting the lessons that life's hardships have taught us. "Living beyond the hurt means embracing the pain, learning from it, and using it as fuel to rise higher than you ever thought possible." It's about acknowledging the hurt but refusing to let it define you.

Turning Pain into Power

One of the most important lessons I've learned is that "pain is powerful, but what you do with that pain is even more powerful." We all have a choice when it comes to how we handle life's hardships. We can let the pain consume us, or we can use it as a catalyst for growth and transformation.

For me, that transformation came when I realized that the pain I had experienced wasn't meant to break me—it was meant to build me. Every tragedy, every heartbreak, every challenge was shaping me into the woman I was meant to become. "Pain is the fire that forges us into the warriors we were always destined to be." And once I understood that, I was able to shift my perspective from one of victimhood to one of empowerment.

The first step in turning pain into power is to change the narrative. So often, we tell ourselves stories about our pain—stories that keep us trapped in the past. We replay the hurt over and over in our minds, convincing ourselves that we are broken, that we are victims of our circumstances. But "you are not a victim—you are a survivor, a warrior, and a creator of your own destiny." The moment you take control of your narrative is the moment you take control of your life.

I began to change the way I talked about my past. Instead of focusing on what I had lost, I started focusing on what I had gained. Yes, I had experienced deep pain, but that pain had also taught me incredible lessons. It had shown me the depths of my strength, the power of my resilience, and the importance of never giving up. "When you shift your focus from what you've lost to what you've learned, you transform tragedy into triumph."

The Power of Positivity and Perspective

Another key to living beyond the hurt is the power of positivity. Now, I'm not talking about the kind of positivity that pretends everything is perfect or that ignores the reality of pain. I'm talking about "the kind of positivity that allows you to see the light, even in the darkest moments." It's about choosing to focus on what's good, even when everything around you feels like it's falling apart.

There were days when the pain felt overwhelming, when it seemed like there was nothing positive in my life to hold onto. But on those days, I made a conscious choice to find something—anything—that I could be grateful for. Sometimes it was something as small as the warmth of the sun on my face, or the sound of my children's laughter. Other times, it was the realization that, despite everything I had been through, I was still standing. "Gratitude is the antidote to pain—it shifts your focus from what's missing to what's present, and that shift is everything."

Changing my perspective also meant letting go of the idea that life was supposed to be easy or free of hardship. For a long time, I believed that if I could just get through the pain, everything would be smooth sailing on the other side. But what I've learned is that life will always present challenges. "The goal isn't to avoid pain—it's to learn how to navigate it with grace, strength, and resilience."

Endurance: The Key to Rising Beyond the Hurt

At the heart of living beyond the hurt is endurance. Endurance is the ability to keep going, even when the road is long, even when the pain is deep, and even when the future feels uncertain. "Endurance is not just about surviving—it's about thriving in the face of adversity."

I've faced many moments in my life where I wasn't sure if I had the strength to keep going. The loss of baby Mario left me feeling like I had been shattered into a million pieces. My diagnosis of multiple myeloma and breast cancer forced me to confront my own mortality. But through it all, I've learned that endurance is about more than just pushing through—it's about embracing the journey, trusting the process, and believing in your own resilience. "Endurance is about finding the strength to rise, no matter how many times life knocks you down."

So how do we develop endurance? How do we cultivate the kind of strength that allows us to rise above the hurt and keep moving forward? For me, it starts with a mindset shift. "Endurance begins with the belief that you are capable of more than you ever imagined." It's about knowing, deep in your soul, that no matter what life throws at you, you have the power to rise.

Endurance is also about self-compassion. It's about recognizing that healing takes time, that growth is a process, and that it's okay to have moments of weakness. There were days when I felt like I was failing, when the pain felt like too much to bear. But in those moments, I reminded myself that endurance isn't about perfection—it's about persistence. "You don't have to be strong all the time—you just have to keep going."

Rising in Life, Business, and Beyond

Living beyond the hurt isn't just about healing from personal pain—it's about thriving in every area of your life. It's about rising in business, in health, in wealth, and in family. "When you learn to live beyond the hurt, nothing can stop you from rising."

In business, I've faced challenges that, at times, felt insurmountable. I've had to make bold decisions, take risks, and navigate the uncertainty of entrepreneurship while dealing with personal struggles. But what I've learned is that the same endurance that helps us overcome personal pain is the same endurance that helps us succeed in business. "Success isn't about never facing challenges—it's about facing them with the belief that you are capable of overcoming anything."

In health, I've had to confront my own mortality, to grapple with the reality of living with a terminal illness. But I've chosen to live beyond the fear, beyond the pain, and to focus on what I can control. "Your health is a reflection of your mindset—when you choose to focus on what you can do, rather than what you can't, you empower yourself to live fully, no matter the circumstances."

In wealth, I've learned that financial success is not just about strategy—it's about mindset. "Wealth is about more than just money—it's about believing in your own worth and having the courage to go after what you deserve." Living beyond the hurt means refusing to let past failures define your future success.

And in family, I've discovered that healing from past hurts allows you to show up more fully for the people you love. "When you heal yourself, you heal those around you." Living beyond the hurt means breaking the cycles of pain and passing down a legacy of love, strength, and resilience to the next generation.

The Power of Living Beyond the Hurt

To every woman reading this, I want you to know that "you are more powerful than the pain you've experienced." You have the strength within you to rise above the hurt, to transform your tragedies into triumphs, and to create a life that is defined not by your past, but by your potential.

Living beyond the hurt is not easy. It requires endurance, resilience, and an unshakable belief in your own power. But I promise you this:

"When you choose to live beyond the hurt, nothing in this world can stop you from rising."

So rise, sister. Rise above the pain, rise above the fear, and rise into the life you were always meant to live. *"Your past does not define you—

Amber Lansdale

Amber Lansdale Coaching
Master Women's Empowerment/Transformational Coach

https://www.instagram.com/Amberlansdale_coaching
http://amberlansdale.com

Amber Lansdale is a women's empowerment/transformational coach, speaker, author, and founder of Her Voice, Her Stage. After overcoming childhood trauma and years of self-doubt, she reclaimed her power, stepping into the bold, unapologetic woman she was always meant to be. Now, she helps women heal, break through limiting beliefs, and take up space—whether in their lives, businesses, or on stage. With a background in healthcare and a master's empowerment certification, Amber combines deep healing work with real-world confidence-building. She's the creator of Her Voice Her Stage and co-host of To.Get.HER podcast, where her and her business bestie, Jeanette Tachynsky, celebrate women rising, thriving, and inspiring. From contemplating her existence to living her best life—traveling, getting married, a bonus mom to three kiddos, leading, and loving fully—Amber is proof that rewriting your story is possible. Her mission? To help women own their voices, embrace their power, and show up in the world as the badasses they were born to be.

Forgiving ME

By Amber Lansdale

At seven years old, I didn't have the words for what was happening, but I knew how to disappear—not from the room, but from myself. That's what trauma does when you're too young to understand it. Your mind finds ways to survive, even when your body can't keep up. It hides in the shadows, suppresses memories, and wears silence like armor.

He wasn't a stranger. He wasn't someone lurking in the shadows. He was an older family member—someone I knew, someone I trusted, someone my family trusted. And that's what made it all the more confusing. We're taught to fear the dark, to lock our doors, to stay away from strangers. But what happens when the person who hurts you is someone you love?

It wasn't violent in the way people often imagine abuse. It was quiet, manipulative, and coated in shame. It stole something from me before I even knew what was being taken.

But it wasn't just the act—it was the silence that followed. I didn't tell, not because I didn't want to, but because I didn't think I could. I was a "good girl." And good girls don't cause scenes. Good girls stay quiet. Good girls do exactly what they're told. I remember him whispering, "Don't tell anyone. No one's going to believe you anyway. It's our little secret." So I kept it. I swallowed the words like poison. That secret became a part of me, a dark, invisible weight that pressed down on my chest every single day.

I grew up with that weight. It shaped how I saw myself and how I let others see me. Even when I couldn't remember everything clearly, I felt the heaviness of it—the confusion, the shame, the self-hatred. I lived in a fog, always wondering what was wrong with me, why I felt broken, why I didn't feel whole.

At times, fragments of memories would surface—small flashes my younger self had desperately tried to bury. I'd push them away, sending them back into the shadows, convincing myself it was all just in my head. How could something so monumental just vanish from my memory? I wondered if I was making it up. Maybe I was just losing my mind. But no matter how much my mind tried to forget, my body never did.

It wasn't until my early thirties that everything came crashing in. I was watching *13 Reasons Why*, a show that dives deeply into the emotional battles teenagers face. When the final episode ended, I shattered. I sobbed uncontrollably, gasping for breath. It was like a dam broke inside me, and all the suppressed memories, all the hidden emotions, came flooding back. And in that moment, I finally said the words I had been too afraid to say: *I was sexually abused.*

That admission changed everything. Suddenly, the depression, the anxiety, the toxic relationships—all of it made sense. The pattern of always chasing love, always trying to earn my worth—it was all rooted in the past I had buried. Naming the abuse was just the beginning. The truth doesn't just set you free—it unravels you. It forces you to examine every part of yourself that you've hidden away.

For a long time, I was tangled in shame. Shame that I hadn't told anyone. Shame that I stayed silent. Shame that I carried the pain for so long. But calling out the shame, giving it a name, was my first step toward healing.

Healing didn't come all at once. There was no single moment when it all got better. It was slow. Raw. Unforgiving at times. However, I found a safe space through empowerment coaching, which gave me tools, rituals, and practices that helped me shift the limiting beliefs I'd carried for decades. It gave me space to speak, to cry, to unravel. And in that space, I began to reclaim the pieces of myself I thought were gone forever—my voice, my worth, my power.

I stopped seeing myself as broken. I began to see myself as resilient. As strong. As a survivor. Not someone ruined, but someone forged by fire, rising from the ashes. I realized I was never the problem. I had just been carrying pain that wasn't mine to carry.

And then came forgiveness.

Forgiveness was complicated. It wasn't a lesson that came easily. The word itself made me sick. I thought forgiveness meant saying what happened was okay—that it didn't matter, that it still didn't hurt, that it hadn't changed my life. But I learned that forgiveness isn't about them. It's about you. It's not about making peace with what they did—it's about making peace with the part of yourself that has carried the pain.

I didn't forgive him. I forgave myself.

I forgave myself for staying silent. For not speaking up. For believing I was broken. For making choices from a place of unworthiness. I forgave the version of me who didn't know better, who thought being a "good girl" meant staying quiet. I found forgiveness in the most unexpected place—in the mirror.

It wasn't about releasing him. It was about releasing myself. Releasing the anger. The resentment. The idea that I had to carry this forever. Forgiveness became my liberation. It was my way of saying, "You don't get to live in my mind anymore. You don't get to dictate my worth."

There were days I clung to the pain because it felt like strength. But pain isn't strength—healing is. Letting go didn't make me weak. It made me free.

Forgiveness wasn't a single act—it was a practice. A choice I had to make again and again. Some days it was easy. Other days, it was the hardest thing in the world. But I kept choosing it. Not for him. For me. Because I was tired of carrying his shadow in my light.

Through healing, I began to dream again. I began to believe in the woman I was becoming. I started to love myself fully and unapologetically. My past didn't define me—it refined me. It gave me purpose. It gave me power.

Empowerment isn't something you find in a book or a podcast. It's something you find within. It's the moment you choose yourself over and over again. It's the moment you stop waiting for someone to save you and realize you've had the power all along.

After I found forgiveness, my life began to shift in ways I had never imagined. I stopped settling for toxic relationships. For the first time, I could see my worth clearly, and I knew I deserved love that was healthy, supportive, and uplifting. I found a partner who loved me—not in spite of my scars, but because of them. Someone who celebrated me for who I truly was and supported my growth. It wasn't perfect—nothing is—but it was real, built on mutual respect and growth.

That love opened the door to so much more than I had ever expected. We created a life together, built on trust, support, and shared dreams. I became a bonus mom to three incredible kids. I embraced my role in their lives, learning and growing with them. My heart expanded in ways I never thought possible. I didn't just gain a family—I became part of something bigger, a loving unit that helped me feel seen and heard, something I had always longed for.

Alongside my personal growth, I built a business that enabled me to empower women the way I had empowered myself. It wasn't just about creating financial independence—it was about showing others that they, too, could break free from their pasts. They could reclaim their power, their voices, and their worth. My mission became clear: to help women rise, step into their authenticity, love themselves fully, and create the lives they deserve. This was more than a career—it was my calling. Every woman who found her power through my coaching reminded me of how far I had come—and how far we could all go.

And then, as if everything was falling into place, I became pregnant with my first baby. The feeling of creating life—of bringing a new soul into this world—was indescribable. I had healed enough to truly embrace motherhood, to step into a role built not on fear or insecurity but on love, trust, and the knowledge that I was ready. The child I carried symbolized everything I had fought for—hope, strength, and a new beginning.

Forgiveness didn't just set me free. It gave me the life I always dreamed of but never thought was possible. It allowed me to heal, to love, to build, and to create a future filled with family, love, and empowerment. And now, as I await the arrival of my baby, I know that everything I've experienced—every challenge, every tear, every moment of doubt—was worth it. I am not just surviving anymore. I am thriving. And the future has never looked brighter.

I started coaching because I wanted to help other women see the power within themselves. I wanted to create a space where they could shed the shame, claim their stories, and rise. I wanted to be the voice I never had. The mirror that reminded them: you are not what happened to you. You are who you choose to become.

I still have moments of doubt. I still have moments when the past creeps in. But now, I meet those moments with grace, with compassion. I know that healing isn't a destination. It's a lifelong journey. Every step I take is a victory.

I'm not a victim. I'm not just a survivor. I'm a woman reborn. A woman who turned her pain into purpose. A woman who stands tall in her truth, who forgave herself, who reclaimed her voice, who is finally—beautifully—free.

And I know now, without a doubt, that my voice matters. That my story matters. And so does yours.

Nakeida T. Edmundson

Founder of G.R.O.W.T.H-Getting Rid of Worry, Trouble & Hurt

https://www.linkedin.com/in/nakeida-edmundson-433a04293/
https://www.facebook.com/nakeida.edmundson
https://www.instagram.com/ms_keida/

Hello, I am Nakeida Edmundson. I was born and raised in Paterson, New Jersey, I moved to Georgia in my early 20's for a fresh start. I am a divorced mother of two awesome teenagers who I adore and love deeply. I am the Founder of G.R.O.W.T.H-Getting Rid of Worry, Trouble & Hurt. I started this organization after going through a very difficult divorce. I wanted to help women who were facing hardship and challenging times, such as divorce or abusive relationships. G.R.O.W.T.H provides mental, spiritual and physical support to women. Helping other women get back on their feet and start afresh is a passion of mine because I remember the help I received when I was at my worst after my divorce. I am currently writing a memoir, and I am so excited to share my story, my journey and my victories.

From Hurt to Forgiveness: My Journey

By Nakeida T. Edmundson

Forgiveness is a journey, and not an easy one at that. During this journey, there will be ups and downs, highs and lows, and times when you will question yourself and your sanity.

I am going to share my journey of forgiveness. I was betrayed and hurt by people who I thought loved me and had my best interests at heart. These were people I called my close friends and family, people who I loved and cared for so much that I abandoned others who did not like them or agreed with my relationship choice. In hindsight, I was very vulnerable and an easy target for manipulation and to be taken advantage of.

I met this man at a time in my life when I was down and out. He said and did all the right things, and I felt comfortable and safe with him. I was quickly accepted and welcomed into his world. Meaning, I became close to his mother and father, and was heavily involved in his church, where the members were like family to him and where he served as a minister. We were married two months after meeting; yes, I know that was very fast. Looking back, it was not one of my best decisions. My family was against me marrying this man so much that my dad refused to walk me down the aisle and give me away, and they objected at my wedding. Yes, I mean they literally stood up right after the minister said, "If anyone sees why this couple should not be married, speak now or forever hold your peace." I was in shock; I had only seen this happen on TV. I felt torn, should I turn around and respond? My future husband whispered in my ear and told me not to turn around; he had me, and it was about the two of us now. Of course, I listened, after all, this man was about to be my husband, my provider, my protector, at least that's what he portrayed, and I believed him. So, the wedding went on because there was no just reason given besides my family feeling that he was not good for me, and that he was not the one I should marry. They must have seen something I didn't see, because they would all turn out to be right in what they were feeling.

Being married to this man started off a little shaky. He couldn't even act right on our honeymoon night. My goodness, he left our hotel suite angry because he had an issue with containing his excitement to the point where he couldn't get excited, if you know what I mean. It wasn't anything that he had to get that upset about. Was this a preview of what he would be like in this marriage? He came to his senses, and we enjoyed the rest of our honeymoon.

The honeymoon phase did not last too long. The infidelity, meeting up with other women, started quickly after we got married. I don't think the ink on our marriage certificate had dried yet. When I tell you that women's intuition is always on point, I also believe that God reveals things to us. Either way, I am thankful for it. Whenever I got the feeling that he was up to something, I was always able to find out what it was. I would find he was emailing women from dating sites, hooking up with women in different cities where he was scheduled to make deliveries for work, or meeting up with random women in the parking lots of stores. When I confronted him about my findings, of course, he denied it. He even got kind of creative (but not creative enough to hide things from me). He would take the battery out of his cell phone and hide it between his weights in his man cave. I guess you could call me Inspector Gadget because I found that battery and would kindly put it back in his phone and see all the text messages he was sending to women. Some would ask, "Why would you go through his phone?" Well, because I wanted to know what he was up to, and I didn't want to be oblivious to what was going on in my marriage. Then came the physical abuse. One instance was when my uncle was in hospice, dying from cancer, my family members and I were there for the last moments of his life. It was very late when I was on my way home, and my car broke down. Another one of my uncles was in town, and he drove me home. Now, for some reason, my husband was very upset. I'm not sure if it was because my car broke down, I was with my family, or it was late, who knows? He picked me up by the collar of my shirt and had me up against the wall, yelling at me. I don't even know what he was saying because I was so focused on the fact that my feet were off the ground, and I was in the air on the wall. He then proceeded to throw me across the room, but thank God, I landed in his recliner. Now, I don't know if that was his plan for me to land in the chair, but I was thankful I did. Another incident was when we were arguing in the bathroom, and he got so mad he pushed me so hard that I flew into the bathtub. I was able to grab the towel rack to stop me from hitting my head, but the force was so hard that when I grabbed the towel rack, it came off the wall. My arm was the only thing injured, and thank God for that. Things could have gone wrong, and I could have hit my head and had a serious injury. God had his arms around me. There was also the verbal and mental abuse, putting me down in private and in front of others. About four years into our marriage, I got pregnant with our son. I was excited and nervous at the same time. His behaviors did not change, and he continued to do the same things, more so when I was on bed rest with my son. I couldn't focus on his stupidity; I had to focus on bringing my baby into this world healthy. I wasn't the happiest in my marriage and was stressed about whether I would be a good mother. I didn't feel like I had the support of my husband, and with this being my first child, I really needed that support. I had support from the people from the church and my in-laws. My son was born a few weeks early, but he was healthy, thank God. When he was five months old, I found out I was pregnant with my daughter. This was a shock, but ready or not, another baby was coming. This thing called marriage was not working out well for me, but motherhood was what made me happy and kept me going. The man whom I rejected my family for did not have my back like he promised at the altar. I was unhappy and found myself putting on a front when we were at church. I found myself taking my own personal communion before church to help me make it through. I would drink quite often to numb my feelings and to cope. I would act as if everything was great in my marriage, so no one would know the truth about their minister. If only they knew what type of person they had in that pulpit preaching to them, they would be shocked.

Although he was sat down several times by the elders of the church, meaning he could not preach for a certain amount of time because of the things that would go on in our marriage and household, that didn't stop him from his lustful ways. It was like a slap on his wrist, and then he would be back preaching as if nothing ever happened. This didn't help me; it was a vicious cycle. We would even go to counseling with our pastor to try to help our marriage get better. Our pastor suggested that we take a day out of the week to go out on a date and enjoy each other's company. That did not work because he would start an argument right before it was time for us to go out, so of course, the date would never happen. However, he made sure to go out several times a week by himself to a lounge. I would offer to go with him, but he never wanted me to go out with him. I got to the point where I didn't care anymore, and I couldn't wait for him to go out after he got home from work. I didn't want to be around him at that point, and I didn't want to be married to him anymore. When we mentioned divorce to our pastor, he told us to go for it if that is what we wanted.

The last straw for me was when I went out of town for a conference for work, and when I returned, he was very paranoid that I was with another man or something. I don't know what was going through his mind. That night in bed, he was very touchy-feely, but I was not feeling him. At this point, I was so disgusted with him and did not want him to touch me. He got so mad that he threw me up against the closet door and started chasing me through the house. I was able to lock myself in the hall bathroom. He began to bang on the door and yell for me to come out. I came out because I did not want my kids to come out of their room. When I opened the door, he told me to leave our house. He opened the door to the garage and yelled for me to get out. Now, our garage had a flight of stairs, and I was so afraid that he was going to throw me down those stairs, that's how mad he was. So, I quickly ran to the front door and left the house. I was so scared; I was outside in the middle of the night, wearing only my nightgown and no shoes. The only thing I could do was walk up and down the street, trying to figure out which one of my neighbors' doors I was going to knock on for help. He shortly came outside and said, "Come back in, I am not going to hurt you." I was skeptical, but I went back inside. We sat down, and he continued to yell about the fact that I didn't want him to touch me, and he wanted to know why. I was so over this, and eventually, he went back to bed. The next day, I left for a couple of days to get away and get my mind together. When I returned home, he had thrown all my clothes into the garage. They were all on the floor, and the rest was packed into suitcases. At that point, I had enough, and we separated. During our separation and the process of our divorce, I received a call from one of the men from our church. He told me that my husband was dating his wife. How long has this been going on? Now, I am still married, and so is the woman he was dating. The woman was from our church, yes, the same church that we both attended, and where he is now an ordained minister, and Reverend is in front of his name. She was someone I considered a good friend. We worked together with the kids in the church, writing speeches and plays. We spent a lot of time together, she was over at my house a lot, our kids grew up and played together, and she even went with me to pick out my wedding dress. Of course, he denied the fact that he had been dating her. I knew there was a reason he was rushing me to sign those divorce papers. During this time, she became distant from me and would barely talk to me or avoid me. That was all because of her guilt. I would catch her looking at him with googly eyes during the church service. But one day, that woman's intuition kicked in, and something made me think that they were married. I called my now ex-husband because our divorce was now final. I asked him if they were married, and he said, "Yes, but don't tell anyone." This was like a gut punch! I was heated! As soon as I hung up that phone with him, I immediately called my mother-in-law. Yes, he said don't tell anyone, but I did not care. Bless her heart, she didn't even know he was married. They went to the courthouse and got married. Now, he hid this from his own mother and church members, the congregation he preaches to. Why did he feel the need to hide this union from the church members? Good question, my guess would be because it wasn't right. When it finally came out, everyone seemed to be okay with it; well, at least it seemed that way. If they did not agree, they did not make it known. I felt so betrayed, and I was hurt that this type of behavior was accepted in the church, in the pulpit. Needless to say, I stopped going to that church. These people didn't care about me or my feelings, like they said they did.

For 16 years, I was married to this man. This is the very short version of what really happened in this marriage. I went through infidelity and abuse. I abandoned my family for him. I struggled with him during our marriage. I birthed his children. We were never able to purchase a home, didn't vacation, or live a comfortable lifestyle. It was always a struggle, and always something going on. It has been several years now since our divorce and his remarrying. He refuses to pick up the phone and call me, all he will do is text me. His reasoning for this is that he doesn't want me to hear me arguing. He treats me like some female off the street or a stranger. The disrespect he shows me is unbelievable. As for her, my so-called friend who befriended me and hung around me was plotting to be around him and to work her way in. I was beyond hurt, of all the women in this world, he chose her, not any of the ones he cheated with that I didn't know, but the one who pretended to be a friend. I had so much hatred in my heart for them to the point where it was unhealthy for me. I developed high blood pressure, gained so much weight, and my self-esteem was gone. At one point, I felt I needed to sit down with the two of them so they could apologize and give me an explanation for what they had done. I wanted to know why they did this to me. I felt this way for a long time until I saw they moved on with their lives, they were living their best life, not giving me or this situation another thought. In the meantime, I'm literally killing myself over a situation that I had no control over, or over a couple of trifling individuals who couldn't care less about me or my feelings. I had to think about saving myself. I had two children who needed me, and I had to be my best self for them. I had to snap out of this funk before it was too late. First, I needed to forgive myself for allowing myself to be hurt for so long and forgetting my worth. Then, I needed to realize they were not going to apologize to me or explain themselves to me because they didn't think they did anything wrong. We cannot expect those who hurt us to be the ones to heal us. If they cared in the first place, they would not have hurt us. I had to find comfort in God and move on with my life. This was a process and a journey for me to get to this point. Understand that forgiveness doesn't mean reconciliation. Some think that you have not forgiven if you do not go back to the way things were with you and that person, or if you don't speak to them again. That's not true; you can forgive and not associate with those who hurt you. You can forgive them in your heart, wish them well, and go on with your life. You will realize you've forgiven someone when you notice you're no longer carrying the same weight, and you feel free. You will be able to look back at the situation and see it as a lesson learned and as a testament for others to see that there is peace beyond the hurt, and you can find forgiveness in unexpected ways.

Nikki Keskula

Founder of The Girl Boss Collective

https://www.facebook.com/GirlBossCollective.net/
https://stan.store/GirlBossCollective

Nikki Keskula is a Massachusetts native, lifelong storyteller, and fierce believer in the power of turning pain into purpose. After spending a decade in the mental health and psychology field, Nikki traded in her clinical desk for a laptop and a bigger mission—helping women build bold, profitable brands rooted in their own lived experiences.

Today, she's an online brand development and visibility strategist who shows up with both strategy and soul. Through her thriving community, The Girl Boss Collective, Nikki empowers women entrepreneurs to share their stories, own their voice, and grow businesses that feel as good as they look.

When she's not mentoring mission-driven women you'll find her outdoors with her dogs and fiancé or curled up with a good book and a cup of tea. Always dreaming, always building, always pushing you to become the best version of yourself.

From Hatred to Healing:
Letting Go of the Unforgivable

By Nikki Keskula

Forgiveness is a strange and complex thing. I can't count the number of times I've heard people say, "It wasn't my intention," or "When are they going to forgive me?" Over the years, I've come to realize that when people ask for forgiveness, it's often less about mending what's been broken and more about soothing their own conscience. They're looking for relief from the guilt that's been weighing on them, hoping that forgiveness will make it easier for them to move on. But the thing is, forgiveness isn't about making the person who hurt you feel better. It's about setting *yourself* free. You don't forgive to ease their burden; you forgive to lift the weight that's been holding *you* down. It's not about condoning what they did or forgetting the pain they caused—it's about choosing to let go of the hold it has over you so you can finally start to heal.

I learned this lesson the hard way, after spending years carrying unwavering hatred in my heart for John, the man who sold drugs to my boyfriend Ben—the drugs that killed him. The same man who, once upon a time, I had considered a friend. The betrayal cut so deep that the grief quickly twisted into anger, and that anger settled into a bitterness that consumed me, and it felt justified. I blamed him for everything, replaying the events over and over in my mind, thinking that holding onto that hatred somehow kept me connected to my loss and gave me some sense of control, some sense of justice. But the truth is, every day I held onto that bitterness, it chipped away at my peace and my ability to move forward.

Forgiving him felt impossible at first—how could I forgive someone who took so much from me? For years, I carried that resentment, convinced that if I ever forgave him, it would be like saying what he did wasn't so bad. But in reality, my inability to forgive wasn't hurting him—it was destroying me. It was my heart that was weighed down, my mind that was filled with anger, and my life that was trapped in that moment of loss. Forgiving him didn't mean I had to absolve him of what he did. It meant that I had to let go of the grip it had on my life, for *my* sake, not his.

I knew the lifestyle that was consuming these guys. Drugs, addiction—it had taken hold of so many people around us, including Ben. But John was my friend, and that's what made it harder. On several occasions, I reached out to John, practically begging him to stop selling Ben drugs. I pleaded with him, telling him that if he truly loved and cared about Ben, he would give him a real chance to get his life together. I knew, deep down, that my words would likely fall on deaf ears, that the addiction and the lifestyle had a stronger hold on John than my pleas ever could. But still, I hoped—hoped that somewhere, somehow, my words would stick and that maybe, just maybe, John would wake up and realize what he was doing—not just to Ben, but to himself. But no matter how much I begged or reasoned with him, nothing changed. And that, too, fueled my anger. I felt helpless, caught between wanting to protect Ben and knowing I couldn't force anyone to change. It left me frustrated and heartbroken, watching as the people I cared about spiraled deeper into a world that I feared would only end in tragedy.

In the end, Ben's chance at recovery slipped away, and I was left carrying the weight of all the "what ifs" that haunted me.

I'll never forget the day after the news of Ben's death. Once the whirlwind of shock and grief from the first 24 hours started to settle, my mind went into work mode. I needed answers—I needed to know exactly how everything unfolded. My thoughts kept replaying the events of that night over and over. I had seen Ben just hours before he died. He had picked me up from my night classes at college to give me a ride home, and the moment I got into the truck, I knew he was high. I was furious. The drive home was terrifying—he kept nodding off at the wheel, and I did my best to keep him alert, trying to make sure we didn't crash. I couldn't believe he would put me in danger like that. That he had lied to me again, that once more, I was dealing with a partner who was high on heroin. The constant rollercoaster of his addiction had become so exhausting. I was trying so hard to get my own life together at this point, and all I wanted was for Ben to do the same. I wanted him to want more for himself, to fight for a better future. What I didn't know then was that Ben had been with John earlier that night. I didn't know that Ben had begged John to front him a $40 bag. And I certainly didn't know that this would be the night when everything in my world would change forever.

I remember the overwhelming relief I felt as we finally pulled into my driveway. I couldn't wait to get out of that truck—to escape the fear, the tension, and the anger that had built up inside me during that terrifying ride home. I hopped out, slammed the door, and walked away, but I couldn't shake the worry that followed me. As mad as I was, I was still scared for Ben and what might happen to him on his ride home. This constant mix of emotions—sadness, anger, worry— had become my new normal, and it was exhausting trying to keep up. Not long after, Ben called me when he got home, apologizing for everything that had happened. He promised, as he had so many times before, that this was it. He was done. He was going to get his life on track. I wanted so badly to believe that this time was different. But a few hours later, something unsettled me. I had a gut feeling that something wasn't right. I was worried about Ben. I thought about calling his brother and asking him to check on Ben, but I held back, not wanting to seem like the "crazy" girlfriend who was always panicking. So, instead, I went to bed. But at 6 a.m., my phone rang. It was Ben's brother, and with a single sentence, my world collapsed: "Ben is dead."

As my mind continued to replay that day and night over and over again, I couldn't shake the feeling that something was missing—

some piece of the puzzle I hadn't yet uncovered. The timeline didn't make sense, and I needed answers. I decided to reach out to John. I needed to know if he had seen Ben earlier that evening while I was in classes. I asked him directly: Had he given Ben drugs that night? There was something that just wasn't adding up. Ben had made it home, he was safe, and he told me he was going to bed to sleep off the high. He had to get up for work the next morning. But something had changed between 10 p.m. and 6 a.m., and I couldn't stop thinking about what had happened in those crucial hours. I needed to know the truth.

John swore to me that he hadn't seen Ben in a few days. He told me that Ben had reached out, saying he didn't have any money and was hoping John would front him a bag until payday. John insisted that he had refused—that he didn't give Ben the drugs. At the time, I wanted to believe him. I clung to the hope that maybe John hadn't been a part of Ben's last night, that maybe there was some other explanation.

I couldn't wrap my head around anything. It felt like I couldn't breathe until I knew every detail of what had happened. The following day, I went to Ben's house, desperate for answers, and found myself in his room with his mother, looking for some sort of clue that could explain how things unfolded. I remember vividly finding a needle full of drugs on the floor, hidden under the carpet. There was also a bag of heroin in his nightstand drawer. The reality of it all hit me like a ton of bricks. I sat on his bed—the same bed where he took his last breath—wondering if he knew what was happening to him in those final moments. Did he lie there, realizing he was overdosing, but was too far gone to call for help? What if I had asked his brother to check on him, would he still be here? The mental torment was unbearable, the questions running through my mind with no way to answer them, and then it dawned on me—I needed his phone. In the chaos of the past few days, I hadn't even thought about it, but the answers I was desperately searching for might be right there on his phone. So, I grabbed his phone and his tablet and rushed home, hoping to piece together the missing hours. But nothing—nothing—could have prepared me for what I was about to find.

Going through Ben's phone was like taking punch after punch to the gut, each revelation knocking the wind out of me a little more. Lie after lie unfolded before my eyes—years of manipulation and deceit laid bare. Ben was living a double life, one that I had seen but was manipulated to believe was all in my head. My heart could barely take it, and yet I couldn't stop. I needed to know the whole truth, no matter how painful. And then, there it was—exactly what I had been searching for. John had lied. He *had* been with Ben while I was in classes that night. They had spent the evening together, smoking crack and shooting heroin. And when Ben left, he took that bag of drugs with him. That was the missing piece—the lie that had kept me from understanding how everything had spiraled so far out of control. The betrayal hit me harder than I could have imagined. John hadn't just lied to me—he had been part of the events leading up to Ben's death. He played a direct role in Ben's final hours, and knowing that, shattered everything inside me.

In a fit of rage, I confronted John. I couldn't believe that he would lie to me about something this important, something that had torn my entire world apart. Ben wasn't just some guy to him—he considered Ben his brother. How could he look me in the eyes and lie, knowing the devastation we were all going through? How dare he withhold the truth from the people who loved Ben, from his family who needed answers just as much as I did? I was furious that he had the audacity to try to protect himself while we were left in the dark, grieving and searching for the pieces to make sense of what had happened. The betrayal was staggering. In that moment, it wasn't just about Ben's death—it was about the cruelty of hiding the truth from those who deserved it the most.

John didn't have much to say when I confronted him. Instead of explaining himself or offering any real remorse, he asked if it would be okay for him to attend Ben's services. The question caught me off guard. In the whirlwind of my emotions, I immediately told him I didn't want him there. How could I? After everything that had happened, how could he think he belonged at Ben's memorial? But ultimately, it wasn't my decision to make. I told him I would ask Ben's parents. To my surprise, Ben's mother, in her deep well of empathy, wanted John to be there. She had compassion for him that I couldn't understand at the time—how could she be so forgiving of the person who played a part in her son's death? It was a level of grace I wasn't ready to give. I was consumed by anger, by betrayal, and by grief. But I respected her wishes. Reluctantly, I told John that Ben's parents had said it was okay for him to come, but I made one thing clear: I didn't want him anywhere near me. I couldn't bear the sight of him, not then, not after everything.

The night of Ben's services was a blur. I stood in line with his family as hundreds of friends, relatives, coworkers, and acquaintances came through to offer their condolences. But the entire time, I was on edge, my eyes constantly scanning the room, waiting for John to show up. He didn't arrive until the very end—just five minutes before the cut-off time at the funeral home. The room had quieted down, and the once-bustling chatter was now fading into the parking lot as people slowly began to leave. For a brief moment, I felt a wave of relief wash over me. Maybe he wasn't coming after all. But then, there he was. John slipped in through the back door, his eyes full of tears, trying to go unnoticed.

I stared at him, and instead of the sadness or compassion I thought might come, all I felt was a deep, burning anger. My blood began to boil, and I could feel my entire body tense. And then I watched as Ben's mother—so full of grace and compassion—walked over to him and embraced him in a long, heartfelt hug. I couldn't stand the sight of it—I couldn't stand to see him receive the forgiveness I didn't think he deserved. Without another thought, I turned and walked away. I had to get out of there before I exploded, before the weight of it all suffocated me.

After Ben's services, my world was flipped upside down. The days and nights blurred together into one long stretch of pain and numbness. I spent most of my time in an alcohol-induced haze, desperately trying to grasp onto anything that might offer even the slightest bit of relief from the overwhelming grief that consumed me. I couldn't believe what had happened—my mind was trapped in a loop of anger, denial, and deep depression. It was all-consuming, and I was spiraling into a darkness so profound that no words could truly capture the depth to which I had sunk. For 2.5 years, I found myself stuck in that place, unable to climb out. I was drowning in my pain, clinging to alcohol as my only lifeline, until one day, I realized that if I didn't make a change, I'd never survive it. So, I made the decision to sober up and start healing.

I began intensive therapy to address my issues with alcohol, my mental state, and the unrelenting grief that had taken over my life. As I slowly began to process my trauma and the immense loss I had experienced, there was one thing I couldn't shake: my anger toward John. Even as the years passed—five years after Ben's death—I was still holding on to that blame for dear life, refusing to let go of the idea that John was responsible for everything that had happened. No matter how much progress I made in other areas of my life, that anger remained, a constant weight on my heart.

I remember the day a friend casually mentioned that John had gone to rehab and had been clean and sober for over a year. "Good for him," I scoffed, bitterness dripping from my words. "Ben should have had that chance, not him." At that point, my anger ran so deep that I couldn't care less about John's recovery. It felt unfair, almost like a slap in the face, that he was given a chance at redemption when Ben never would be.

One of the 12 steps of recovery is making amends to the people you've hurt, and when my circle of friends began telling me that John had reached out to them to make his amends, I couldn't help but wonder when it would be my turn to hear from him. But the message never came. I felt like the dragon on top of the mountain that he had to slay—the one he was too afraid to face. For over a year, I heard nothing from him, and it only deepened my anger. Did he not realize the destruction he had caused in my life? Did he not understand how much he had taken from me? It was like throwing gasoline on the fire of my hatred, thinking that everyone else deserved an apology, but somehow I wasn't worthy of one. And then, on the day before the six-year anniversary of Ben's death, I got a message on Facebook. It was from John, asking if we could meet for coffee and talk.

The message came early that morning, and I stared at it in disbelief. After all these years, I never thought John would confront me, and yet there it was—his words on the screen, asking for a conversation I wasn't sure I was ready for. That entire day, I couldn't stop thinking about his message, playing it over and over in my mind. How should I respond? In the heat of the moment, my first instinct was to lash out, to finally release all the anger and hurt I had bottled up. But I had grown so much over the years. I wasn't the same person I was when Ben died, and I had learned through my own healing process not to react impulsively, especially when emotions ran high. I wanted to take some time to truly sit with my feelings, to understand what I needed to say, and to make sure my response came from a place of thoughtfulness, not just raw emotion. I knew that once I responded, it could open doors I wasn't sure I was ready to walk through. This wasn't just about him—it was about my own healing, and I wanted to make sure I handled it with the care it deserved.

I knew that seeing John face-to-face was not something I was ready for. The thought of sitting across from him, confronting all the emotions I had been carrying for years, felt overwhelming. But I also realized it was time to face the music and finally hear what he had to say. So, later that evening, after much thought, I responded to his message. I told him plainly that I wasn't ready to meet in person and didn't believe a face-to-face conversation was the best approach for us right now. However, I was willing to listen to whatever it was he needed to share. It was a step, a small one, but it felt like the right way to move forward—on my terms, at my pace.

John respected my decision and responded with an apology that I could tell was long overdue. He opened up about his struggles, his deep regret over how everything had unfolded, and how he wished more than anything that he could go back and change things. For the first time, I could feel the sincerity and remorse in his words. He wasn't just apologizing for my sake—he had clearly been carrying the weight of his actions for years. He shared how hard he had worked to turn his life around, how he had taken the broken, shattered life he was living and slowly glued it back together, piece by piece, into something he could finally be proud of. It wasn't an excuse for what had happened, but it was a glimpse into the pain he had been living with, and I could sense that his transformation was real.

I responded to his message with sheer honesty, something I hadn't allowed myself to do in years. I told him how Ben's death had shattered me, how much pain I had been carrying around for so long because of everything that had happened. I admitted that for a long time, I had blamed him entirely for Ben's death. But after years of self-reflection and long nights filled with tears, I realized something that had been difficult to accept—Ben's death wasn't John's fault. Ben had made his own choices that night, and while John had been involved, Ben would have made those decisions regardless. For so long, I needed someone to blame, and because John was still here while Ben wasn't, it became easier to place all my anger, my hurt, and my grief on him. I couldn't talk to Ben, couldn't rage at him for the decisions he made that led to his death, so I directed it all at John. And that was wrong of me.

For the first time, I began to understand the compassion that Ben's mother had for John. She saw something I couldn't for so many years. I let him know that I had carried an immense amount of resentment toward him for the past six years, and that while I wasn't yet at a place where I could fully forgive or release all the hatred in my heart, I wanted to get there. I wasn't ready to let go completely, but this was a step in the right direction—one that I knew was necessary for both of us to begin healing.

The following day was the six-year anniversary of Ben's death, and for the first time in what felt like forever, I felt lighter, more at peace. It was as if a weight I had carried for so long had finally started to lift. I was proud of the way I handled my conversation with John. For the first time, I allowed myself to see the situation for what it truly was—complicated and painful, but not insurmountable. Life has a funny way of bringing things to you exactly when you need them most, whether it's a blessing or a lesson. And this? This was a lesson, one that I would carry with me forever. It taught me that forgiveness isn't about absolving someone of their wrongdoings; it's about finding the strength to release the grip of pain and resentment for your own healing. As I reflected on the journey I had been on, I realized that this conversation wasn't just about John or Ben—it was about me, about reclaiming my peace and moving forward with grace.

After our conversation, I didn't speak to John again. I watched his life unfold from a distance on social media—years of sobriety, a beautiful daughter, and a life he had worked so hard to rebuild for himself. I couldn't help but feel proud of him. Turning his life around took a kind of strength that most people don't have, and it was clear that he had done the work to create something meaningful out of the wreckage.

It was three years after that conversation that John and I would finally meet face-to-face. A mutual friend of ours had passed away unexpectedly, and as I approached the services, I knew John would be there. I had no idea how things would go. It had been nine years since I had last seen him—since the night of Ben's services—and I wasn't sure what it would feel like to confront all the emotions that had lingered since then. But I knew this moment was inevitable, and part of me was ready to see how far both of us had come.

As I walked out of the funeral home, I saw a group of our old friends gathered in the parking lot. And there he was—John. He looked good, healthier than I had ever seen him, with a glimmer in his eye that reminded me of the boy I knew before everything went wrong. He wasn't the same person I had been angry with for so long. I knew he wouldn't be the one to approach me, and before I could think too much about it, my body just took over. I walked over to him, without hesitation, and gave him a hug. I asked him how he was doing, and we exchanged a few small pleasantries. It was surreal, but that moment was bigger than the words we were saying. Then, I looked him in the eyes and told him that I was proud of him. His eyes filled with tears, and he quietly said, "You don't know how much that means to me." And in that moment, I knew—I had forgiven him. The weight I had carried for so long lifted, and I felt a peace I hadn't felt in years. It was a quiet, simple exchange, but it was everything I needed to finally let go.

I never saw John again after that day. As I sit here now, writing these words, it's just 24 hours after hearing the heartbreaking news that John took his own life. The beautiful life he worked so hard to build— gone in an instant. It's devastating to think that, despite all the progress he made, he still succumbed to his inner demons. He fought so hard for his sobriety, for his family, for his future, and he deserved to see it through. The weight of this loss feels heavy, not just because of who John was, but because of everything he overcame, only for it to end this way. It's a sobering reminder of the invisible battles people continue to fight, even when it seems like they've won the war.

John's life was a testament to both struggle and resilience. He lived through the darkest of times, made unimaginable mistakes, and yet found the strength to rebuild from the ground up. He fought battles that most of us will never understand, and though his story ended far too soon, it's important to honor the life he lived—the one he worked so hard to create. John wasn't perfect, none of us are, but he showed that it's possible to rise from the ashes and strive for something better. I'll remember him for his determination, for the strength it took to fight his demons, and for the brief but profound moment of peace we shared when I finally forgave him. His life, though marked by tragedy, was also a story of redemption, and I hope that's how he's remembered—as someone who, despite everything, tried to make things right. Rest in peace, John. You deserved more time.

J.J. Mathieu

Author and Astrologer

https://www.facebook.com/jjmathieuauthor
https://www.instagram.com/j.j.mathieu/

J.J. Mathieu is a writer, astrologer and full-time mom with a background in corporate and academic Communication. She earned a Master's Degree in Communication Studies from the University of Rhode Island and is a graduate of Debra Silverman's School of Applied Astrology. J.J. has been writing in a variety of contexts since she was a child crafting fiction books with pencil and spiral-bound notebook in hand. She has worn many hats during her career, but all have centered around or have been influenced by her love of writing. J.J.'s work has appeared on The Barre Blog and MomsIntoFitness.com. Her personal challenges serve as the foundation of her writing, which focuses on inspiring others to see their own lives through a lens of deep compassion and love for themselves and others. In addition to writing, J.J. loves reading, baking, mindful movement and anything chocolate and sparkly. Connect with J.J. at jjmathieuauthor@gmail.com.

Divine Intervention

By J.J. Mathieu

It's been almost two years since I typed the words "The End" on the final page of the first draft of the very first book I ever completed – a sweet and wholesome romance novel. I had been dreaming of this day for a very long time, wondering what it would feel like to type those magical words at the end of the longest manuscript I'd ever written. Tears filled my eyes as I realized I had not only completed a book, but a lifelong goal – to actually write a book. I leapt up from my desk chair and raced downstairs to our media room to tell my husband the good news. I was literally jumping with joy as I shouted the words, "I did it! I finished my book!" I floated around my house for the entire rest of that evening and into the next day before the reality of my situation actually took hold. Despite the fact that I had just pushed through the last two months of daily word counts, internal roadblocks and juggling my writing time with my stay-at-home mom duties, the external problem that had been plaguing my household, as well as my marriage, was still there and would stand in the way of me ever turning my draft into a finished novel.

For the sake of divulging too much information and for the privacy of the other individual involved in this delicate situation, I will spare you the details of the actual problem, which I will heretofore refer to as "the setback." All that really needs to be said is that it was a long-term setback that ebbed and flowed. It had been ebbing and flowing for a few years, and when things were good, my mind, body and soul were at ease. When things weren't good, my creativity took a hit, and I couldn't concentrate on transcribing the crystal clear visions swirling around in my head onto the page. As I had been taught to do, I decided to let my first draft rest for a while so that I could give myself a break from it, as well as the tiresome task of actually completing a first draft. I planned on letting the draft, as well as my mind, percolate for a few months before tackling the editing phase. I was signed up for an editing course that was set to begin in January and felt confident that taking the summer off to spend with my two daughters would be the break that my mind and creativity craved.

Before I knew it, the hot summer sun began to fade into its autumnal glow. The setback that I had been dealing with was stable, as we had been consulting with a professional to help on the home front. I coasted through the holidays as the excitement about my upcoming editing class began to replace the predictable post-holiday lull. January dawned fresh and new, and I joined my fellow classmates – those who had also completed their first drafts of their books alongside me several months earlier – as we dusted off our manuscripts and readied ourselves for the polishing stage of the book-writing process. *"This is it,"* I thought to myself. *"Within the next couple of months, your book will take shape and come to life. By the middle of this new year, your draft will officially be a bright and shiny book ready to be shopped around or self-published."* The familiar burst of joy that I had experienced that previous summer rushed back full-force and propelled me through that first month of the class.

Then, everything stopped short. It happened again. The setback was back. My creativity slid into its hiding place as my mind raced, trying to figure out how to deal with the setback's latest appearance. My draft sat partially polished as I made excuse after excuse as to why I couldn't continue on with the editing process. My mentor knew of the problem and what I was dealing with inside and outside of myself, and she gave me the support and grace that I desperately needed. I mustered up enough strength to finish attending the actual editing classes themselves, but like it did during the most festive months of the year, my manuscript sat collecting dust once again.

I was beside myself with grief and loss as I tried to tend to the situation at home, along with the ache that accompanied the disappointment I felt towards myself for not completing my book.

Friends and family would ask how my book was coming along, and all I could do was answer with the same fabricated justification that I had come up with during those difficult times:

"Things got very busy at home with the girls, and that left little time for writing. I hope to get back to the book when our schedule calms down a bit more."

Thankfully, my lame excuses were always met with sympathetic, yet understanding, nods. But, as with everything else in life, things didn't calm down – they only got worse. I found myself torn between my responsibilities to my family and my deep-down desire to be a published author – to share my words with the world and to somehow brighten at least one person's day with my story. I was sad, lonely, depressed and more distraught than I ever thought possible. I did everything that I could think of to fix the setback at home – group therapy, one-on-one counseling, and sharing my anguish and pain with my close family members. But, nothing could lift the fog that had taken up a permanent residence in my heart and mind. I was desperate to try anything, and then fate intervened.

I can't remember exactly when I got the email from Hay House, but it came at the perfect time for me, as we like to say in the metaphysical world. It was an advertisement for a free class on journaling with Oracle cards with Colette Baron-Reid. I had been journaling on my computer for the past several months as a way to sort out all of the tangled thoughts in my head. Some days, the words flowed from my fingertips like a rushing river. Other days, I had to force myself to type those few remaining words to hit my daily journaling word count goal. My emotions were all over the place, and I knew that my writing reflected this, but I also knew how much it helped just to get those musings down on the digital page. Learning a new technique for journaling – one that would help guide my writing intuitively – sounded like the exact thing I was looking for.

I signed up for the free class and loved it so much that I ended up purchasing the actual course and dove straight in. I flew through the course and became absolutely enthralled with Colette's writings, teaching style and philosophy. Her method of journaling with Oracle cards allowed me to synthesize many of the feelings that I'd been having since the setback had entered my world. For the first time in a long time, I was able to write again. And not just type, but handwrite the actual emotions that I'd been grappling with for so, so long. As my thoughts spilled out onto the pages of the pretty notebooks that I purchased specifically for my journaling, and my cursive handwriting improved, so did my mindset. My heart began to heal, and I felt more like my author self again.

Since learning from Colette brought me so much inner peace, I began listening to her YouTube videos on a regular basis. I was obsessed with this new way of using Oracle cards and wanted to gain as much knowledge from Colette's unique interpretations and processes as possible. It was during one of Colette's Cards and Stars videos that I was introduced to her good friend, Astrologer and Therapist Debra Silverman. *"Hmm...,"* I thought to myself. *"Cards and Stars. That's an interesting combination."* Since I was a child, I have always been interested in astrology. I was the eager student who checked out all of Seymour Simon's books on the planets from the library, asked for a telescope for Christmas (and subsequently dragged my dad down to the freezing garage to set it up as soon as I could) and lived and died by the horoscope books that I bought at Waldenbooks during my teenage years. I had to know more about Debra Silverman and her Applied Astrology School and how it might help me overcome my writing blockages.

Coincidentally, or maybe not-so-coincidentally, Debra's school was hosting a free four-day astrological immersion at that exact moment that I discovered her. I ended up logging on during the second day of the immersion and was immediately entranced by her teachings. I had tried to learn astrology on my own before, but it just seemed so confusing to me. The planets, the signs, the houses and all of those symbols and red and blue lines were just too much to absorb without some sort of easy-to-digest, applicable system. And that's exactly what Debra and her school offered. I was hooked and knew that I needed to know more. Debra's school promised that you'd walk away from her curriculum knowing your soul's promise, your life lesson and how to fall in love with your true self – all of the things that I knew I needed to learn in order to heal my heart and find my way back to my writing voice.

I enrolled in Debra's Applied Astrology School in July of 2024, during the peak of the setback at home, and left the rest up to fate. Like I had done at the beginning of the year, I told myself that in six months – by December of 2024, I'd know more about astrology, myself and the world around me. Secretly, I also hoped that not only would I gain a better understanding of myself, but also of my husband. I so desperately longed to forgive him for the problems that we had been experiencing over the past few years and knew that the solution was in the stars.

I dove into my astrological studies with the rigor of an Olympic athlete and wasn't surprised to find that, like Colette's teachings, Debra's really resonated with me. The truth is, I've always felt different than others around me. I've always been interested in the metaphysical world and have allowed my intuitive hits to guide me more times than I often admitted to others. When I thought about what really spoke to me regarding my own healing, tools such as Oracle cards, crystals and essential oils appealed to me more than group therapy. Before I really leaned into my metaphysical persona, I had extensively studied aromatherapy and crystal healing and became a Clinical Aromatherapist and Advanced Crystal Master two times over. I've always felt very drawn to Mother Earth and more organic styles of healing. Learning about astrology really helped tie everything together for me. In a matter of eight months or so, I went from stressing out over all of those squiggles on a natal chart to feeling a rush of excitement surge through me whenever I pulled a new natal chart up on my screen. I soared through Levels 1, 2 and 3 of Applied Astrology, made new astrological friends and found my calling – one that would allow me to use my newly acquired astrology skills and my author voice, which had finally found its way back to me.

And in the middle of all of my studies with the stars, the setback that had been plaguing my homelife and my marriage began to dissolve. By letting go of the situation, which I forced myself to do by becoming so deeply involved in my astrological studies, things came to heal on their own. As I took the steps toward becoming a proper astrologer and learned more about my soul's curriculum, as Debra promised, I began to fall further in love with myself – the good and the not-so-good – and eventually came to forgive myself for the setback that I'd been dealing with at home. Additionally, I forgave myself for countless other traumas that I had experienced during my 46 years of life. Things that I had always blamed myself for – my melanoma skin cancer diagnosis in 2003, an early miscarriage in early 2008, the loss of my son due to a non-malignant brain tumor during his 19th week of gestation in late 2008, my subsequent two high-risk pregnancies in 2009 and 2012 and my eventual autoimmune disease diagnosis in 2016. The weight of guilt that I had been carrying around with me for my entire life (which can also be explained by my astrological blueprint) fell to the wayside, allowing for a sense of airiness that I'd never experienced before.

In addition to forgiving myself, I was also able to forgive my husband. Once I studied his chart and learned about his own soul's blueprint, I fully understood why he had also been suffering all of these years. I have a greater knowledge of his life lesson, his communication style and his soul's purpose. Because I learned how to read his natal chart, I now have a much deeper compassion for and appreciation of the man I married. And the setback that had been plaguing my household? For now, it's a thing of the past. Well, actually, upon further investigation combined with some composite natal chart magic, I've learned that the issue we'd been fighting all of this time was written into our relationship's soul curriculum. But now I have the tools and foresight to navigate the situation with a bit more ease as my husband and I continue our journey through life together.

To say that astrology saved my marriage as well as my sanity is an understatement. Because I finally learned how to decode and decipher all of those funny-looking glyphs, shapes and colored squiggles on a natal chart, I have a greater understanding of myself, my husband and my children (another story for another anthology!). I am grateful that astrology allowed me to forgive myself, as well as others, for something that I might not have had the strength or fortitude to forgive in the past. I've spent so many years trying to figure out what makes others tick, especially those that I love the most. I majored in Communication in both college and graduate school because I've always had this deep need to understand the motivations of others. However, it wasn't until I learned how to read a natal chart that I could fully comprehend the intricacies of the human psyche.

Perhaps this chapter wasn't what you expected. It wasn't a revealing tell-all regarding a very private and personal setback that I lived through over the course of the last few years. But I didn't intend for it to be. I wanted this chapter to reflect the positive, healing side of being able to forgive and to move beyond the hurt. I wanted it to demonstrate the transformative power of what it feels like to walk through the glowing embers of a raging inferno, to be reduced to a pile of ashes and to rise from those ashes stronger and more confident than ever before. We've all walked through our fair share of infernos and have more than likely pondered who was to blame. During the weakest points of my life, I fell to my knees begging for an answer to the ever-lasting question, "Why me?" It took me 46 years of inquiry and eight months of astrology to learn that the answers have been above me all along. I just didn't have the right map to find them until I cast my own natal chart for the first time. Today, my natal chart is a living, breathing illustration of my life's purpose and my soul's promise. And even though I can't change the planets' positions at the time of my birth or the way they continue to dance around the Zodiac on a daily basis, I do have free will to take all of that planetary energy and use it to craft the life and stories I truly desire – all thanks to a little starlight as my guide.

Mariana Alvarez

Founder and CEO of Controller Works

https://www.linkedin.com/in/mariana-alvarez-268269208/
https://www.facebook.com/profile.php?id=100091949612677
https://www.instagram.com/controllerworks2023/
https://controllerworks.com/

Mariana Alvarez was born and raised in a small town of Sao Paulo, Brazil, with a childhood rooted in a sense of community and the constant seek for education and improvement. After obtaining a bachelor's in business administration and a Master of Science in Accounting in the USA, she endured a challenging divorce but found the strength to protect her children and rebuild her life. Despite setbacks, she persevered to establish Controller Works, a virtual outsourced accounting firm dedicated to supporting small to mid-size family-owned businesses. This venture not only represents a business pursuit but also provides fulfillment as it allows Mariana to assist other small business owners in achieving their goals and creating legacies for their families. Her individual experiences have fueled a determination to heal from past trauma and positively impact the success and growth of other family-owned businesses. Through Controller Works she seeks to build a dedicated team to offer virtual accounting support to small business owners, empowering them to progress, realize their aspirations, and establish enduring legacies for their families. Mariana enjoys technology and works diligently on staying up to date on the newest tools that allows her to increase efficiency and automate processes. During her free time, Mariana enjoys spending time with her daughter working on puzzles, reading, and exploring the world through traveling.

Sacred Release:
A Journey Through Forgiveness and Freedom

By Mariana Alvarez

Have you ever found yourself at a crossroads, grappling with the weight of past hurts and wondering if true freedom is possible? The journey of forgiveness is rarely straightforward, often leading us down unexpected paths of self-discovery and healing. In this chapter, I explore the transformative power of forgiveness through the courageous report of my own story as I navigated its complex terrain.

This narrative offers more than just a tale of reconciliation; it provides a beacon of hope for those still finding their way through the darkness of resentment and pain. As I delve into these accounts, I'll uncover the unexpected ways forgiveness can manifest in our lives, reshaping our perspectives and opening doors to personal growth we never thought possible.

Forgiveness, I've learned, is not a passive act—it's a courageous rebellion against the pain that seeks to define us. My journey through betrayal, trauma, and ultimately healing taught me that forgiveness is rarely about the other person. It's about choosing ourselves, reclaiming our voice, and refusing to let past wounds dictate our future. Through my spiritual journey, I discovered that forgiveness is not linear—it's messy, often unexpected, but deeply liberating. In sharing my story, my hope is to shine a light on what becomes possible when we choose to release bitterness and open our hearts to the uncharted terrain of healing.

The Unexpected Shift: Turning Pain Into Purpose

Life has a way of throwing curveballs when we least expect them, and sometimes these unexpected events become the very catalysts that propel us towards forgiveness and growth. For many, the journey begins not with a conscious decision to forgive, but with a sudden realization that change is necessary for survival and growth.

I was a successful entrepreneur on the outside, but behind closed doors, I was trapped in a 17-year marriage defined by control, emotional abuse, and escalating violence. The most extreme act came one night when, during an argument, he struck me so hard that he broke one of my teeth. I remember the shock more than the pain—the moment everything I had tried to suppress became impossible to ignore. But what finally broke me wasn't just what he did to me—it was when his violence began spilling over to our children, especially our daughter, and the almost drastic incident when he struck her cellphone with a hammer right out of her hands. That was my moment of clarity. In the midst of fear and chaos, I found a strength I didn't know I had. It was that strength that pushed me to finally leave, to protect my children, and to begin the long and painful journey toward healing and forgiveness.

This unexpected awakening became the catalyst for my own journey towards forgiveness, with not just of the abuser, but of myself for staying in the situation for so long. As I took the brave steps to leave that marriage and protect our children, I also began the arduous process of self-forgiveness and healing.

My story is proof that forgiveness often begins in the most unlikely circumstances. For me, it wasn't a gentle epiphany—it was a jarring, painful realization that forced me into action. Walking away from a life I had built over nearly two decades was terrifying, but staying would have cost me even more. In choosing to leave, I wasn't just saving myself—I was showing my children the value of self-respect and the transformative power of reclaiming our lives. My resilience became their anchor, and through that, I began to understand what forgiveness could really look like: not forgetting, but choosing to move forward without allowing the past to define us.

Redefining Strength Through Vulnerability

In a world that often equates strength with stoicism—where holding back tears is seen as composure, and silence in the face of pain is mistaken for dignity—the act of forgiveness challenges us to completely redefine what it means to be strong. Forgiveness isn't passive. It's not a weakness. It requires us to confront the rawest parts of ourselves, to lean into the discomfort of our wounds, and to let go of the armor we've carried for so long. For many of us on the path to healing, it's in that exact moment—when we finally allow ourselves to feel, to grieve, to speak the truth—that we discover a deeper strength. Embracing vulnerability doesn't make us fragile; it makes us human. And in that humanity, we find a well of power and resilience that we never knew existed. It is through that openness, that brave, unguarded space, where forgiveness begins to take root and where true transformation becomes possible.

For most of my life, I took pride in my emotional control and fierce independence. I was the one who always held it together, who didn't cry, who pushed through pain without asking for help. So when I was betrayed in one of the most personal and devastating ways, my first instinct was to shut down—to bury the hurt and keep going as if nothing had happened. But eventually, the weight became too heavy to carry alone. I decided to seek help from a therapist and started opening up to her. What I discovered in those conversations surprised me: True strength wasn't in pretending I was fine—it was in allowing myself to be vulnerable, to be seen in my brokenness. That honesty became the turning point in my healing. It was through that raw openness that I found the courage to forgive and begin putting the pieces of my life back together.

This vulnerability opened doors to unexpected connections and support. By allowing others to see my pain, I created space for genuine healing and forgiveness to take root. I learned that forgiveness wasn't about forgetting or excusing the actions that hurt me, but about freeing myself from the burden of resentment and negative emotions.

Through this process, I began to redefine my understanding of strength. I had spent so many years pretending everything was fine, convincing myself that burying the pain made me stronger. But the truth was, it took far more courage to face my hurt head-on than it ever did to suppress it. Acknowledging my pain, speaking it out loud, and allowing myself to feel it fully—that was the real act of bravery. This newfound strength, born from vulnerability, became the foundation of my journey toward forgiveness and self-discovery. It was in those moments of honesty with myself that healing finally began to take root.

The Ripple Effect of Self-Forgiveness

One of the most profound and often unexpected aspects of the forgiveness journey is the impact of self-forgiveness. Many embark on this path focusing on forgiving others, only to discover that the most challenging—and rewarding—act of forgiveness is directed inward.

For me, the hardest part of the journey wasn't walking away from the abuse—it was facing myself in the quiet aftermath. I had spent years internalizing the blame, convincing myself that I had somehow allowed it to happen, that I should have seen the signs sooner, acted faster, been stronger. Even after leaving and rebuilding my life, a part of me carried shame, not just for what I had endured, but for how long I had endured it. That shame became a heavy shadow, one that followed me into new chapters, whispering that maybe I wasn't as strong or as wise as I tried to appear.

It took time—years, honestly—to even realize how cruelly I was treating myself. I would never have spoken to a friend the way I spoke to myself in my thoughts. I had to unlearn the lies that had taken root in my mind and heart. Forgiving myself wasn't a single moment of clarity—it was a series of quiet decisions: to speak kindly to myself, to honor the version of me who did the best she could with what she had, and to acknowledge the courage it took just to survive. I began to realize that holding myself hostage to the past wasn't justice—it was self-punishment.

And something beautiful happened when I softened toward myself: the way I showed up in the world began to shift. I found it easier to connect with others and hold space for their imperfections because I had learned to do the same for mine. That ripple effect of self-forgiveness extended to my parenting, my friendships, and even my work. By releasing the weight of self-blame, I opened the door to deeper compassion—not just for myself, but for everyone around me. I learned that true freedom doesn't come from forgetting the past—it comes from forgiving ourselves for how we carried it.

Forgiveness as a Journey, Not a Destination

One of the most crucial realizations on the path to forgiveness is understanding that it's not a one-time event, but an ongoing journey. This perspective shift can be both challenging and liberating, as it removes the pressure of achieving a perfect state of forgiveness and instead focuses on the process of healing.

After going through a painful divorce, I initially believed that forgiveness meant wiping away all the negative feelings I had toward my ex-husband. I thought that if I truly forgave him, I wouldn't feel angry or resentful anymore. So, every time those emotions came up—which they often did—I felt guilty. I'd tell myself I must not have healed enough or that I was failing at forgiveness altogether.

As I deepened my spiritual journey and began reconnecting with my inner self, I came to a powerful realization: carrying those negative feelings wasn't just holding me back emotionally—it was weighing on me spiritually. Resentment, anger, blame—they all had a way of clouding my energy, dimming my light, and disconnecting me from the deeper sense of peace I was searching for. I realized that every time I clung to those emotions, I was keeping myself tethered to a past I desperately wanted to move beyond. My spiritual practice became a guidepost, reminding me that forgiveness was less about letting anyone off the hook and more about liberating my own soul.

That change in mindset allowed me to be gentler with myself. I began to recognize and celebrate the small victories. I stopped chasing perfection and started embracing the reality that forgiveness is a path I walk every day. And with that came a quiet kind of freedom—the freedom to grow, to feel, to forgive at my own pace.

Forgiveness Through the Eyes of Others

Some of the most powerful lessons in forgiveness have come to me from the most unexpected places. And perhaps the most profound came from my own daughter. For years after leaving the abusive marriage, I carried not only my own pain but an unbearable weight of guilt for what my children had endured. No matter how much healing work I did, there was always a part of me that questioned whether I had done enough—whether I had protected them soon enough, spoken up loud enough, or left fast enough.

One day, in a quiet moment I'll never forget, my daughter looked at me and said, "All that happened to us was not your fault, Mama, you should not blame yourself for it." I was amazed. I hadn't even realized she carried that clarity, let alone the grace to help me free myself from that guilt. Her words pierced something deep inside of me—both shattering and healing me.

In that moment, I saw forgiveness in its purest form—not as something earned, but as something freely given from a place of deep empathy and love. Her words gave me permission to start forgiving myself on a new level. I realized that forgiveness isn't about rewriting the past or denying the damage—it's about choosing to release the power that pain has over our future. Through her, I began to see that healing doesn't always come from within—it sometimes arrives through the people who love us enough to show us what's possible.

The Unexpected Freedom of Letting Go

One of the most profound and often unexpected outcomes of forgiveness is the sense of freedom it brings. Many embark on the journey of forgiveness, focusing on the other person, only to discover that the greatest liberation occurs within themselves.

For a long time, I carried the weight of my trauma like a shield. I told myself that holding on to my anger and resentment was a way of honoring what I'd been through—a form of justice, of not letting my abuser get away with it. The idea of forgiveness felt like betrayal. I believed that if I forgave, I would be letting him off the hook, excusing what could never be excused.

But as I started working through my healing—both in therapy and through my spiritual journey—I began to see the truth more clearly. Diving into spiritual growth and studying the laws of God helped me understand that holding on to anger wasn't serving justice; it was chaining me to the very pain I wanted to escape. My resentment wasn't punishing him—it was punishing me. The emotional weight I carried was affecting every part of my life, while he continued on, untouched by the suffering I kept reliving. I began to understand that God's law isn't about revenge—it's about release, redemption, and reclaiming the life we were created to live. And in that truth, I saw that forgiveness wasn't weakness—it was a sacred act of obedience, and ultimately, liberation.

Forgiveness and Holistic Well-Being

We often hear about the emotional and psychological healing that comes with forgiveness, but what truly surprised me was how deeply it impacted my physical health. I never expected that releasing emotional pain could bring such real, tangible changes to my body. But as I began letting go of anger, guilt, and resentment, I started to see just how connected our emotional well-being is to our physical state. The more I forgave, the more I healed—not just in my heart, but in my whole body.

For years, I struggled with chronic stress that showed up in my body in ways I couldn't ignore—constant migraines, stomach issues, fatigue that no amount of rest could fix. I went through countless medical appointments, tried different treatments, and changed my diet, but nothing seemed to bring lasting relief. It wasn't until I started to confront the unresolved anger and resentment I had been carrying that I began to notice a shift—not just emotionally, but physically.

As I leaned deeper into the process of forgiveness—toward others who had hurt me, and even more so toward myself—I began to feel the weight lift, not only in my heart but in my body. My migraines became less frequent, down to none. The knots in my stomach began to ease. I started waking up with more energy, more clarity, and a sense of calm I hadn't felt in years. I realized then how deeply our emotional wounds can affect our physical health, and how healing one often means healing the other.

As I felt lighter emotionally, something beautiful began to happen— I started finding joy in moving my body again. I found strength I didn't know I had and began to reconnect with my health in a new, empowering way. Exercise became not a punishment or a chore, but a celebration of how far I had come. I craved nourishment, movement, and care—not just as a routine, but as an act of love toward myself.

This transformation didn't just feel miraculous—it made perfect sense. Through therapy and my spiritual practice, I came to understand the intimate connection between the mind and body. Letting go of bitterness and blame didn't just lighten my spirit—it gave my body room to heal. Forgiveness became more than an emotional release; it became a path to holistic well-being. And in that process, I learned that peace isn't just a feeling—it's something we can live in, breathe in, and feel in every fiber of our being.

Embracing the Ongoing Nature of Forgiveness

As I close this chapter, I'm reminded that forgiveness hasn't been a single choice I made one day and never looked back on—it's been a journey, one that continues to unfold in layers. Some days, it's easy to feel peace and closure. Other days, old wounds resurface when I least expect them. But I've learned that these moments aren't failures—they're invitations to go deeper, to reconnect with the healing that's already begun, and to give myself grace along the way.

Forgiveness, especially when rooted in deep pain, isn't always clean or easy. Sometimes, it feels like crying in the middle of the night, and other times, like laughing again without guilt. It's forgiving others, yes—but even more often, it's forgiving myself. For staying too long. For not knowing better. For carrying the shame that never belonged to me in the first place. With each step forward, I reclaim more of my voice, my strength, my joy.

My hope is that my story, along with the reflections I've shared, offers you something real—whether it's comfort, clarity, or simply the reassurance that you're not alone. Forgiveness doesn't mean forgetting or pretending it didn't happen. It means learning to accept what did happen and choosing to stop carrying it as your identity. Through my spiritual journey, I've come to understand that every painful chapter held a lesson—an invitation to grow, to deepen my faith, and to become the woman I was meant to be. By turning inward, by seeking God's guidance and reflecting on those lessons, I've begun to transform my wounds into wisdom. Forgiveness, for me, became a sacred tool for healing—not because it changed the past, but because it gave new meaning to it. And in that meaning, I found peace, purpose, and the freedom to move forward with grace.

Martha Smith

Martiem.smith.com
Top International Resilience Ambassador |
Award-Winning Author | Inspirational Speaker

http://linkedin.com/in/martie-smith-8b062025
https://www.facebook.com/martie.smith.37
https://www.instagram.com/martiem.smith
http://martiemsmith.com/

Martie M. Smith is a U.S. veteran, 4x best-selling author, and globally recognized resilience expert and ambassador. From mechanic to mentor, her journey reflects unwavering courage through adversity—transforming caregiving, surgeries, and reinvention into a purpose-driven mission.

Her books, including Creative Chaos Warrior and She Wins, share powerful stories of healing, leadership, and growth. With authenticity and heart, Martie inspires people of all ages to embrace their truth and rise stronger.

🏆 Honors & Awards
- Certified Personal Trainer (2023)
- ICWP International Woman Educator Award (2023)

- Heart of Gold, Resilience, and Humanitarian Awards (2024)
- Star Educator & Tenacious Educationist (2024)
- SWUSA Global Leadership & Keynote Speaker (2024)
- Top Resilience Ambassador & Inspirational Icon (2025)
- Force Magazine Top 10 Entrepreneurs (2025)
- Brainz 500 Global Leader & Senior Contributor

⟡ *"Writing is how I honor resilience."* —Martie M. Smith

Between Two Worlds – Until I Rebooted: CTRL + ALT + REAL

By Martha Smith

"I had tasted both worlds yet lived fully in neither. Passion, purpose, and mission called to me—but I moved through life like a candle without flame, vision blurred, direction lost. I wasn't just stuck... I was unseen by the very spark I longed to ignite."

We often arrive at our defining moment not in triumph but in tension—between who we've been and who we're becoming.

That quote? It wasn't just a line I wrote—it was the mirror I faced. The ache of living in pieces, playing roles, dimming my light to meet the needs around me. Maybe you've felt that, too. You're caught between doing and being, expectations and truth, survival and significance.

This chapter is the story of when I stopped ignoring that quiet inner tug and finally pressed **CTRL + ALT + REAL**. Sometimes, life doesn't need a reinvention—it requires a reconnection.

CTRL: When Life Demands a Hard Pause. I had spent decades in service, leadership, caregiving, and creation. Each title I wore added to my identity: veteran, mechanic, author, educator, daughter, survivor, resilience coach. But titles can also become disguises when they no longer reflect your truth.

Storm after storm hit. Losing jobs. Enduring surgeries. Caring for my father during Alzheimer's and my mother during cancer and holding it all together while silently falling apart.

I remember standing in a hospital corridor, phone in one hand, responsibility in the other, and my spirit somewhere between. I whispered a silent "CTRL" to God, life, and myself.

"Pause me before I forget who I am." Because I wasn't just tired—I was disappearing.

ALT: The Alternative Path Nobody Talks About. The World teaches us to keep pushing. But healing doesn't come from hustle. It comes from honoring our heart's truth.

I had followed the rules, served with discipline, reinvented endlessly— but it felt like I had lived 49 lives in 49 cities and still hadn't landed in the one that felt like home.

So, I stopped asking, "What's next?" and began asking: "What's real?" "What's worth rebuilding?" "What could I do if I were not afraid to start over?"

I realized that the alternative path isn't failure—it's freedom. It is the choice to walk away from a life of survival into one of significance, to choose truth over trophies, to follow peace, not pressure.

REAL: Reconnecting with What Can't Be Downloaded. I had become an expert at showing up strong. But strength without joy is exhaustion in disguise.

So, I went inward. I asked my younger self what she needed. I let the woman I had become cry in places I used to perform. I deleted outdated beliefs and downloaded new courage.

That's when I met my spark again—not the performative one that smiles on stage, but the one that dances barefoot in the kitchen, writes stories by moonlight, and heals others by living her truth out loud. The one that finally said:

"No more diluted versions of me. It's time for the real thing."

When the Reboot Began, the unraveling didn't happen all at once. It was slow, like a leak in my soul. Drip by drip, I was losing parts of myself I didn't even know I had misplaced.

And then—one ordinary morning—I broke. Not loudly. Not publicly. But in the quietest, most personal way, I couldn't answer the question, "What do you want?"

Not what I should do. Not what was expected. Just—what did I, Martie, want?

Silence. That question echoed in the hallway of my heart with no response.

That's when I knew something sacred had been lost—not my ability to give, strength, or connection to self.

And so began my reboot—not because I had a grand plan, but because I had reached emotional, spiritual, and physical capacity.

I didn't need another achievement. I needed a reset. I needed to find the original spark—before trauma, before roles, before expectations piled on top of my essence.

I sat in my car one day, after another exhausting caregiving appointment, and whispered: "God, I don't know what to do anymore. But I'm ready to find out who I am now."

That was my CTRL. I looked at my life and chose the alternative: a life not built on proving my worth but on protecting it.

And slowly, like spring thawing a long winter, I remembered what joy felt like. Not performative happiness—but soul joy. To write just for me. To dance with no audience. To say no and not apologize. To grieve what I lost without guilt. To wake up not with dread but with curiosity.

That... was my REAL. And that's when the sparks started returning.

Realign. Reignite. Reboot. Rebooting doesn't mean scrapping everything. It means rescuing the most sacred pieces of yourself from the wreckage and rebuilding from truth, not trauma.

That's what I did. That's what I do.

I began to write the stories that were buried under my silence. I started to coach from the inside out—not from a script, but from scars. I began to build a life that didn't just look resilient—it felt aligned.

I stopped fearing disappointing others and started fearing what would happen if I kept disappointing myself.

And here's what I learned along the way:

- You can be successful and still feel starved.
- You can be admired and still feel invisible.
- You can be strong and still feel like giving up.

But when you choose to reboot? You stop surviving. You start becoming.

The Spark They Can't Download

I didn't climb out of the storm—I learned how to dance in the rain. I didn't escape the chaos—I let it reveal what I was made of. I didn't just survive—I rebooted.

Every time I felt lost, I returned to this truth: They can replicate your work, borrow your words, and mimic your methods—but they can't download your spark.

My spark wasn't built in applause. It was forged in adversity, tested in silence, and refined in fire.

And no system, no trend, no title could ever replicate that.

So, I stopped waiting for permission. I rebuilt my life from the inside out, word by word, choice by choice, spark by spark.

And here's the beauty: I didn't become someone new. I returned to the version of me I had buried beneath obligations and expectations.

Your Reboot Invitation Now, I turn this chapter into a mirror. Look into it and ask yourself: • What if the spark you're looking for... is already within you? • What if you're not broken—just buried beneath burnout and borrowed expectations? • What would your life look like if you press **CTRL + ALT + REAL**?

Maybe your reboot starts with one hard truth, one brave decision, or right here with these words: "I'm ready to remember who I am."

Let that be enough for today. Because when you begin again—not with force, but with fire—you don't just rewrite your story. You reignite your legacy.

The Final Note: There's a reason you're still here. A purpose that keeps tapping your shoulder when the world gets too loud. A mission waiting for you to say yes to yourself.

So, if you've tasted both worlds—achievement and emptiness, strength and sorrow—and still feel like you've never fully lived... It's not too late.

Reboot. Realign. Reignite. And when you do—don't just show up. Shine so fully that even your shadows find the light. Because this time... You're not just surviving the storm. You're becoming the lightning.

What No One Sees Behind the Smile There's a version of me most people see—the one with the polished words, the empowering message, the steady presence. The one who's coached hundreds, written books, stood on stages, and smiled through it all.

But what they don't see? They don't see the nights I sat on the bathroom floor, praying to a God I wasn't sure was still listening. They don't see the days I performed strength while silently wondering how I'd keep going. They don't know the grief I carried in my lungs while leading others to find theirs.

Behind the smile was exhaustion, behind the encouragement was emptiness, and behind the productivity was a person on the edge of burnout.

But I've learned this: Hiding behind your smile is a survival mechanism—not a shameful act.

We smile to function, to hold it together, to protect others from what feels too heavy. And yet, healing begins the moment we let someone in, when we say, "I'm not okay, but I'm here," when we allow the smile to drop and let the truth rise.

The smile served me. But it also silenced me.

So, I had to make peace with the pain behind it—not to get rid of it but to integrate it. I had to honor the resilience it took to smile in the storm and the bravery it takes now to live beyond it.

Because the real power isn't just smiling through the storm. It's learning to speak through it. And in that truth-telling, we don't lose strength—we multiply it.

Legacy Reboot: The Spark of Ms. E.

Let me tell you about Ms. E. She was 76 when I met her—graceful, sharp-witted, and unapologetically honest. On the outside, she was a retired schoolteacher with silver hair and hands that looked like they had prayed for generations. But on the inside? She was a woman who had just begun again.

After losing her husband of 50 years and watching her grown children build lives far from home, Ms. E. felt invisible. "Like an extra in a movie I used to star in," she told me once.

Her days had become quiet, predictable, and gray.

But one morning, she woke up and whispered the exact words I once had: "This isn't it."

She pressed her version of CTRL. She paused the autopilot routine of empty mornings and silent dinners. She began asking questions she hadn't dared to ask in decades: "What makes me feel alive?" "What legacy do I still want to create?" "What if my best chapter is still unwritten?"

Then came her ALT. She altered her input. She joined a creative writing class at the local library. She started journaling. Then storytelling. Then mentoring. She swapped reruns for poetry nights and silence for soulful conversation.

And the REAL? It came when she stood up during a local open mic and read one of her stories aloud. Her voice trembled—but her truth didn't. She shared her grief, her joy, her wisdom. And in doing so, she lit a spark in everyone listening.

Within a year, Ms. E. was running intergenerational writing circles. Children, teens, adults, and elders sat in the same room, learning how to tell their stories to the world. Her living room became a sanctuary of second chances.

She told me, "I didn't reboot to be someone new. I rebooted to become who I almost forgot I was."

That's the power of legacy. Not what you leave behind—but what you ignite while you're still here.

Ms. E.'s spark wasn't loud or flashy. It was steady, sacred, and real. It reminded me that it's never too late to reinvent yourself or inspire others to do the same.

A Call to the Legacy Leaders

Whether you are 18 or 88, this moment is your invitation. Not to hustle harder. Not to chase someone else's version of success. But to build something lasting—something aligned with who you truly are.

A legacy isn't just what you leave behind when you're gone. It's what you live while you're here. It's in the stories you tell. The truths you speak. The sparks you pass on—through your actions, healing, and presence.

So, if you're still breathing, you're still building.

To the youth: You don't have to wait until you've "figured it all out." Start now. Start messy. Let your curiosity lead. Ask questions that shake rooms. Be bold enough to build differently.

To the elders: You're not too late, tired, or behind. Your wisdom is medicine, your resilience is a map, and your voice is the blueprint someone else is praying for.

To the middle-of-the-road warriors—those balancing caregiving, careers, quiet dreams, and loud doubt: You are the bridge between generations. Don't underestimate your power to reset cycles and replant purposes.

You are not defined by the storms you've endured—but by the strength you chose to summon afterward.

Legacy doesn't require perfection. It only requires presence. Intention. Love.

So, whether your spark has just been lit or burning for decades, let this be your reminder: Your light is needed. Your story matters. Your reboot can ripple through generations.

Build what only you can build. Shine how only you can shine. And leave not just a mark—but a movement.

Legacy isn't found in the spotlight but in the spark you refuse to let go out.

A Final Blessing To You—Reader, Warrior, Spark-Bearer

May you remember what the world made you forget. May you rise not with pressure but with peace. May you walk into your next chapter carrying only what's sacred.

May your healing echo into generations not yet born.

I bless your courage to pause, your audacity to reboot, and your heart's willingness to be seen not as perfect but as present and real.

Let every no you speak protect your yes. Let every boundary you set rebuild your belongings. Let every tear water something beautiful in you.

You are not behind. You are not broken. You are blooming—in your own divine time.

And as you go forward, may your light shine and ignite others to remember theirs.

Because this world doesn't just need you here, it requires you whole.

With gratitude for your journey, with reverence for your spark, and with faith in all you're becoming—

With fierce love,
Martie M. Smith Resilience Ambassador | Creative Chaos Warrior

Abigail Sikes

Forgiving Gifts, LLC

https://www.linkedin.com/in/abigailsikes
https://facebook.com/purposefulhealing
https://www.instagram.com/forgivinggifts
https://forgivinggiftswellness.com/

Abigail Sikes RN, BSN CS. She is a Registered Nurse, Amazon Best Selling Author, Entrepreneur, and Life and Forgiveness Coach. She is the Owner and Founder of Forgiving Gifts LLC. With 25 years of nursing experience and currently holds a position as a Post Acute Care Nurse at Penn Medicine. She is very active in the community and currently serves as President of the Minority Nurse Educators of Chester County, Oversight committee member for the Equity Health Center, and Health Coach for the Art Holding Hands and Hearts (AHHAH) Stand Up Stand Out (SUSO) program.

Forgiveness Is the Key to Wholesome Living

By Abigail Sikes

What does it mean to forgive, and why is it important? Are there benefits to forgiving those who have hurt us? Are there benefits to forgiving ourselves?

Studies have shown that people who forgive live healthier lives physically, mentally, and spiritually. I believe in the power of forgiveness and its ability to change lives forever. But how do I know this, and why do I have such conviction in it?

I had to reach deep within and find my healing after a failed relationship. I had to realize that the responsibility to heal rests with me. My thoughts would determine my future, not those of someone else who didn't live in my shoes. I had to understand that I would never have a constructive future if I did not heal from my past. The Holy Bible says, "As a man thinketh in his heart, so is he" (Proverbs 23:7).

The day I discovered my purpose and the solution to life's challenges was when I accepted that I was in pain and consciously resolved to move forward.

But I was not always forgiving. I had trouble being forgiven of anyone who hurt me. That crippled my development and kept me emotionally, physically, and psychologically stunted. Though I am a nurse and aware that forgiveness is vital to health and well-being, I still struggled with letting go of the past and didn't want to own what I was feeling. It was much easier to disregard the negative feelings and pretend they didn't exist. Everybody else was always responsible for where I was.

I learned lessons about forgiveness when I was a young woman who watched my mom suffer with demons from her past because she could not forgive those who hurt her. I eventually lost her to cancer at the tender age of fifteen. That should have been my most significant clue, but it wasn't.

Had I only understood that God puts challenges before us so that we can learn the lessons, find our purpose, and lead the rest of our lives helping others, I could have entered the road to recovery much faster than I did. I wasted a lot of time and energy asking irrelevant questions about emotions and tears that did not heal or change what had already been done.

I also believe that there is the right time for everything. I count the wasted time as a blessing because I can now share and help as many people as possible, so they do not make the same mistakes I did. An attendee at a seminar I recently gave remarked that I must have had some serious therapy to reach this stage in my life. I took that to mean that he recognized that I had come a long way and was a true survivor. I smiled silently, accepted the gift of words he was conveying, and told him I welcomed the journey because it prepared me to share the blessing of forgiveness with everyone. This is my truth!

The day I found my purpose, I really wasn't looking for it. I was looking for relief from the emotional hurt I was feeling, to move forward in life, to stop being stuck with negative thoughts in my head, and to find peace of mind. I'm going to share my thoughts about that day in the hope that you will understand that it's when you hit rock bottom that the only place you can go from there is up!

One night, as I wrestled with sleep again, I sat on my bed with thoughts of finding out more about my ex-husband's affair. Thoughts of feeling worthless and that God didn't love me were going around in my head. I progressed to thoughts of feeling that I was better off dead.

It was about 10 o'clock at night, and when I could no longer stand my thoughts, I got up from my bed and went into the bathroom. By this time, tears were pouring down my face, so much so that I struggled to remain quiet and unheard. It was as if the tears themselves were taken over by another force because no matter how hard I tried to stop, I couldn't. Eventually, I felt myself give in, become uninhibited, and speak from my soul.

I know that the bathroom is the last place you should pray in, but this is where I was, and there was no stopping it. *"Lord,"* I said in hoarse whispers, *"I have had it, I have had it. I am sick of this, and I cannot take it anymore. These negative, hurtful thoughts are on my mind when I go to bed at night, when I get up in the morning, and frequently throughout the day. You must help. I want to move forward. I deserve to be happy. You must help me move my hurt, anger, and negative thoughts."*

I held onto the sink for support, saying words I had never uttered. I cried before. I had admitted to being in pain before, but I had never openly affirmed that I wanted to move forward, that I wanted to be happy, or even that I wanted the pain and negativity to go away. I continued, *"Lord, I have wanted to forgive him from the beginning. You know that I had this in my heart from day one. I forgive him, my Lord, I forgive him."*

By this time, I was crying so hard, speaking with such energy that my grip on the sink tightened, and my body stiffened as I sobbed from the depths of my soul until I thought the sink would give way and rip from the wall.

Water is cleansing, and as if on cue, I resolved to cleanse myself of everything that was weighing me down. I removed my clothes and got into the shower with tears still running down my face. I cried a lifetime's worth of tears. I bathed myself that night as if I was determined to rid myself of every ounce of sadness that ever entered my soul, and I continued until the sobs reduced to a lesser calm.

I would dare to say that God spoke to me in those moments, and I know that that would be quite a claim, but I strangely felt as if He had heard my plea because the tears stopped, the cloud lifted from my head, and my heart felt openly positive. When that happened, I had an epiphany of ideas. I had a conversation with myself that I can liken to no other discussion I have ever had.

"I want you to put a Forgiveness program together. I want you to teach people how to forgive. I want you to approach members of the church, share useful topics concerning depression, stress, anxiety, opioid addiction, and food addiction, and demonstrate how it relates to the inability to forgive. Include the children in the program through play because it will also empower them. I want the focus to be about showing the relationship between being unforgiving and how illness can take over our bodies when we harbor past hurts and resentment."

Do you know the feeling of renewed purpose? That's exactly what I got from that meltdown because when I got out of the shower and walked back to my bedroom, it was with a hurried sense of purpose. I remember thanking God for every step I took, and when I got into bed this time, I still couldn't sleep. I was too excited about my ideas, and I could not wait to begin my mission. The truth is that when we shift our thoughts from helping ourselves to helping others, we find our purpose and therein lies our true healing.

I learned two important things from this experience:

Prayer is good, but lifting the curtain between you and God is imperative. Talk to Him about your joys and fears openly, but make sure to be specific about what you want.

Live with renewed faith daily that whatever you want will come your way, even if the answer is no. God knows what is best for us; if the answer is no, there is always something better that He has planned for us. Remember the keywords *"prosper, hope, and future"* always, and remind yourself of them whenever you feel down.

I started the process of healing the day after my epic meltdown. I approached my church elders and found excellent support from them. From my pastor to my colleagues, everyone bought into my ideas and encouraged me. We split the responsibility for educating the community about various topics and began sharing and bringing people on the journey of lasting forgiveness and healing.

There are so many memorable events that stand out to me. They have contributed to my growth and joy in re-inventing myself. I shed all inhibitions and self-limiting beliefs and went on to write a play and a song for the children to perform, direct, prop, choreograph, and deliver to an open-minded, open-hearted audience.

Discovering this new journey was just the beginning, and I wanted to see the program go further. To do that, I knew that the program had to become sustainable, so I established Forgiving Gifts. This is a small business where I sell little mementos that remind people about healing and forgiveness. The proceeds help us take our message further with musicals, dramas, seminars, and workshops. The book you are now holding is a part of the Forgiving Gifts initiative, and I fervently hope the message will spread far and wide.

The truth will always set you free. It has certainly set me free of my concerns, depressive thoughts, sleepless nights, anxiety-driven journaling, and, most importantly, pain. I am living my purpose in absolute joy because when I help others, my soul is calm, relaxed, and content. God is great, and I challenge anyone to tell me He doesn't exist!

I learned important lessons from this experience. The first is that we need to forgive past events and accept that they happened to teach us lessons and prepare us for a better future. The next is that when we forgive the people who have hurt us, it ought to be unconditional. We should not accept them back into our lives when it is dangerous for our future, but letting go of their actions frees us of the burden we carry from unanswered questions. Then, we ought to acknowledge our errors and the part we may have played in whatever went wrong with our lives. We were the decision-makers, and we allowed what happened to us. Forgiving ourselves for those decisions is essential in healing and moving on. We must work on being *empathetic*. Walking in other people's shoes is key in giving us different perspectives and makes us more tolerant and less judgmental. When we become more tolerant, we learn to think before we respond, and we should always respond rather than react. Reaction brings more conflict, and more conflict brings more unease. The last one on the list is loving ourselves. Yes, we deserve to be loved, and it all starts with having forgiving and kind thoughts about ourselves, taking care of our health, eating well, exercising, sleeping, and pampering ourselves.

The most important thing that came out of this journey is that I have changed the team I play for. I no longer play for the losers who put me down and have no belief in me. I play for the side in which I am my biggest fan and have conviction in myself.

My story didn't begin and end in the bathroom the night I had all these epiphanies. It started there and survived because:

I have a mission that is important enough for me to achieve. I appreciate myself and others and am excited about life and my daily mission. I have conviction in myself and envision the results of this incredible journey I have been entrusted with. I constantly leave my comfort zone, do things that make me happy, and push the boundaries. I respect myself and love the color of my skin, my curves, and my hair. I'm beautiful, and I own it. I go to sleep with a clear conscience because I champion forgiveness. I love God and am grateful for His presence in my life.

I am on Team Gail because I see value in supporting, inspiring, motivating, and loving myself. I am my favorite person in the whole wide world. What team are you on? My book, *Purposeful Healing,* is where I share my story and have helped multiple women heal, find inner peace, and move forward through forgiveness.

Ellen Arsulic Forbus

Founder of Strategically You
Coach

https://www.strategicallyyou.biz/

Ellen Arsulic Forbus is a native of Northeast Ohio, has two sons, a fabulous daughter-in-law, and a precious grandbaby. Her career in financial services has spanned over 40 years, where she empowered clients to reach practical solutions to financial stability and security. Ellen became a certified life coach in 2014. These skills also aided in better relating to her customers and their money mindset. Ellen's coaching focuses on navigating life by knowing yourself better. Having lived through many pivotal moments, she looks for the lesson in each, whether good or bad. You can't see the good in things when pain still lingers. Acknowledging and moving forward are part of life and promote healing. Ellen's ideal clients are women in their 40's or greater who is struggling to fit in as her world changes. She has experienced trauma in life and desires to feel vibrant and comfortable in her changing roles.

My Father's Eyes

By Ellen Arsulic Forbus

What if you woke up one day and found out that almost everything you ever knew or were told about yourself was a lie? A big, fabricated story with intricate layers so heavy and thick that you looked in the mirror to see if you were still the same person you were yesterday.

Sure, there had been a few hints over the years, but very few. The biggest clue came twenty-five years prior, and you vetted it out with the family matriarch before dismissing it.

That warning was received when your youngest son was nine years old and had just joined a new tournament baseball team. Your husband took him to his first practice and stuck around to watch, as the team and coaches were totally new, so he wanted to get a feel for everything instead of just dropping him off and leaving.

The only other parent to stick around struck up a conversation with him, beginning with the pleasantries of getting to know each other. "How old is your son? Where do you live?" And many other pieces of information were exchanged. At one point, you tell the woman your wife's maiden name and where you live. She grew up in the same house you now live in, and her family was known by many in the area, even though her father had passed away right after her high school graduation.

The woman pauses, then blurts out, "She could be my sister!" She then begins to weave a story so fabulous, your husband couldn't wait for practice to be over so he could run home and rub it in your face – or so it seems when he excitedly starts giving you the low down while you're trying to get the kids their dinner.

"What sister, Mom? Didn't know you had a sister!" said one son. "I don't!" I shot back as I grimaced at my husband and told him this conversation could wait. My heart was racing, and I had no idea what he was talking about. Could my dad possibly have cheated on my mom? Could I have a sister through his indiscretion? My dad did not seem like that type. He was a lot of things, but not a cheat or liar.

After the kids were in bed and we were up in our bedroom, he told me the whole story. Apparently, when this woman was a little girl, her *dad* used to bring her to my house and sit her down to play while he and my *mom* went off. A few months later, he brought her by once more, and there was a baby in the bassinet that he showed her. He asked her if she wanted a little sister. She didn't have too much else to add, as she was just a young child at the time, around four years old.

Thoughts were zipping through my head. MY MOM? My mom was always so dramatic and anti-sex, I couldn't imagine her doing anything like what was described. So, I took it to the matriarch – my aunt Eva.

Eva was one of my dad's older sisters, and she was a straight shooter. She did not mince words, nor did she play the fool. She told it like it was and stomped off. A true Croatian in temper and smarts.

Dad's family was 100% Croatian – they came here around 1907 with their oldest son, then had nine more children, my dad being the youngest. They were proud, hard-working, and somewhat socially backwards. Probably growing up on a farm in the twenties and thirties, trying to learn English and fit into the American culture, had something to do with that.

I was nervous. How do I approach Eva? I knew I had one shot. Eva and her sister, Helen, used to come over on weekends, and when there was baseball, which was about six and a half days a week, they would sometimes come over afterwards and join us for dinner. One particular night after dinner, I asked Eva to take a walk with me in the field, on the premise of checking out the blackberry bushes, to see if the berries were forming yet.

We started off towards the bushes, and when we were out of earshot of everyone, I began my story. Eva was pretty stoic, so it was difficult to tell how she was processing this. When I finished and waited, it seemed like an eternity. When she spoke, she was stuttering her words.

"We-we-well, that woman was awfully young, who-who-who knows where she really was or wha-wha-what she saw!" She finally stammered. Then, she sealed it with, "Besides, you look like your father." And that was the end.

I did ask her not to say anything to my mom. Again, Mom could be a little dramatic, and this would send her into a great tizzy. I wouldn't be able to trust her to come to another of my son's games, because she would try to find out who was saying this and then probably have a major meltdown and embarrass me and my family.

That was the last time that was ever spoken about it, until I joined my oldest son and his wife twenty years later in doing an ancestry test. My son popped up as a 50% child, but the others who gradually filtered in on my DNA relative list were names I'd never heard before.

At the time, that made sense. My mom was also from a large family; she was the baby of thirteen, and several of her brothers were married several times and had kids from various women. So, it would not surprise me to have all these unknowns, especially since I knew a few of the women changed the last names of their children after divorcing her brothers.

But on July 4th, 2022, I was sitting on my deck scrolling on Facebook when I got a friend request from that woman who my son had played baseball with. She never approached me with the story, and we became baseball parents who attended many games together over the years our sons played on the same team.

I gladly accepted the request, then had a weird feeling. She, like many women, used their maiden name as her middle name on her Facebook profile. I stared at that name, and then it hit me. At least twenty people on my Ancestry DNA match had the same name!

I sat there for the longest time, not sure if I was going to vomit or not, my whole body shaking. After a bit, I thought to send her a private note on Messenger.

The note began, "Twenty-five years ago, you told a story, and some things popped up recently in my life. I need to know more...

Then, I waited.

It took hours for her to respond. I wasn't sure if she had not seen it yet, or was too shocked to reply, or what the delay was, but it seemed like weeks went by before I heard the "ping" on my phone.

The next few months were so difficult for me. I felt like I didn't know who I was. I had no identity. I had always enjoyed talking about and was proud of my dad's side of the family, of my Croatian heritage. Heck, I even took two trips to Croatia to meet the descendants of those who stayed behind.

I was a fraud. An imposter. That's it – I had the original imposter syndrome! I was lost. Devastated. The days and months and years of lies all came flooding back. The layering, to keep everyone fooled that I was truly my father's child.

My big brown eyes. How many times had I heard that from my mom, "You've got your father's eyes." Sometimes, it was said sarcastically, because my dad could throw a mean look, and so could I. I sat there and wondered, who did she really mean when she said I had my father's eyes?

It took about four months for me to get over the shock. I remember going to my oldest son's house a few days later, and he and his wife could tell something was wrong. They hounded me to confess, as they thought perhaps I had a health issue and was trying to figure out what to do. When they found out, they were shocked, too, and very sympathetic. My daughter-in-law was very practical, and she pointed out that I was now missing half my medical history. I was so in shock that I woke up on their couch the next morning. I must've fallen asleep, and they knew I needed a place where I belonged, so they covered me up and let me stay.

My sister, on the other hand, handled the news extremely well. She was thrilled to have another sibling. She, we, I guess, have an older brother. Unfortunately, he passed not long after I found out this news.

I asked my newfound sister to give me some space, as this was quite a shock to my system. It wasn't her – she was more than welcoming.

It was me.

I now felt such a stigma. I felt betrayed. Lied to. Unwanted.

So many memories came flooding back, and those helped to keep me in this new purgatory I found myself in.

Stories that my mom told me, like how when she was six months pregnant with me, my dad came home drunk and tried to drown her in the laundry sink. She started premature labor and almost lost me.

Unwanted. For the first few years of my life, I don't remember my dad having much to do with me. Prior to this, it didn't bother me. But now, was he staying away from me because he was ashamed of me? It was not my fault. All I ever did my entire childhood was to make him proud. And I could never seem to accomplish that. Now, it makes sense as to why.

His drunken rages made sense now, too. He was self-medicating. He was a spurned husband whose wife cheated on him and had another man's baby, and he was angry and did not know how to deal with it. I couldn't blame him, yet I could.

He used to come home so drunk and beat my mom black and blue. Why didn't he just kick us out? Why the brutality? It wasn't just mom getting hit; it was an innocent little child taking a gut punch every time she heard screams, slaps, thuds, and more. It was a little girl trying to process why life was so chaotic.

Since all the guilty parties were now deceased, I could do nothing but draw conclusions from the little information I knew and the memories I had.

Perhaps the night Dad tried to drown Mom was the first time he heard about her being pregnant from another man.

Another story my mom used to tell me is that after I was born, Dad left the hospital, then came back the next day, drunk and bloody. He was throwing a fit at the hospital and almost had to be removed. After my parents divorced, my dad and I frequently fought. I was not going to let him bully me like he did my mom. One of the times I was staying with him after a long separation, he asked why I was mad at him. I brought that story up and said, "Why did you go to the hospital when I was born and raise so much hell?"

He looked at me, directly into my eyes, and, after a long pause said, "I was at the bar celebrating your birth, and some wise ass asked me if you looked like me or Charlie."

After a moment, but still staring hard into his eyes, I countered with, "Who IS my father?" Dad paused for an uncomfortable pause and then said, "Well, you look like me. You've got my eyes." And that was it.

Charlie! That name. That moment with my dad came back to me. I messaged my new sister and asked her what her father's name was. A short time later came the reply. Charlie!

A few days later, she messaged me a picture of my dad sitting on a picnic table with her brother, and she is standing nearby. The top of the table was filled with strawberries. My dad and her dad had taken them to go strawberry picking. They were friends? That made it worse. WOW!

The memories kept coming. I made several trips to the cemetery to cry, scream, and yell at my parents. At each visit, I told them that I loved them, that I know shit happens, but why did they have to screw me up so bad? Why did they take their issues with each other out on me – not directly, but indirectly? I was collateral damage.

The fact that my life suddenly made sense was also scary. I never felt like I belonged. My cousins have regaled me with stories about my parents and how fun and loving they were when my cousins were little. They talk fondly about how my dad would get down on the floor and play with them. These aren't the parents I knew or grew up with.

While my dad's drunken beatings of my mom were wrong, I could sympathize with him. He was like a wounded animal. How devastating to his pride. And my mom was the love of his life. To have that love betrayed. Dad died right after I graduated from high school. His alcoholism consumed his liver, and his heart gave out.

My mom always made Dad the villain. I used to hate him when I was younger. It was his alcoholism that ruined our lives. His abuse that made me a cowering little girl, never coming out from behind my mother's skirt.

This life-changing secret happened three years ago now. I am still dealing with the fallout of emotions and memories and feelings. However, I have reconciled with my parents. I love them both and know that they were both a product of their time and upbringing, and I don't feel either had emotional maturity.

Healing

I have immersed myself in literature on childhood trauma, a topic that is increasingly recognized as a profound influence on both children and adults who have endured adversity in their formative years. It's remarkable how the universe delivers fragments of wisdom just when you need them most. Shortly after my discovery, I listened to a podcast by Dr. Gabor Maté. His story struck a chord with me and illuminated aspects of my own journey toward healing.

Dr. Maté was born in Hungary in 1944—a perilous time for Jewish families in the region. In a desperate bid to ensure his survival, his mother gave him up after his birth, and he never met his father. Though he reunited with his mother as a child, his tale of absorbing the negative energy of his prenatal environment resonated deeply with me. Experts often advise expectant mothers to create nurturing atmospheres through calming music and positive surroundings. But for Dr. Maté, still in the womb, the love and safety that should have enveloped him were absent. Similarly, I realize now that my own earliest moments were shadowed by chaos and fear.

When my father attempted to drown my mother while she was six months pregnant with me, her nervousness and stress became the backdrop to my prenatal world. Coupled with heavy smoking and my father's likely drunken tirades filled with verbal abuse, the turmoil created an environment devoid of peace. What an introduction to life—a womb steeped in discord and pain.

The more I delved into the literature on childhood trauma, the more I recognized my own behaviors and tendencies reflected in the experiences of others studied. In 2014, I became a certified life coach. Part of this journey stemmed from my need to rebuild my mental and emotional health, even before I fully understood the truth of my childhood. My coaching pursuits gave me a platform to help others, particularly some of my financial clients, while also embarking on my own healing journey.

Before uncovering the depths of this truth, I understood the importance of personal development—working on thoughts and habits is essential, akin to exercise for the mind. This inner work keeps us healthy and engaged. But once I grasped the reality of my early experiences, it became clear that the universe had been gently preparing me for this revelation all along.

Over the years, I journaled extensively about my childhood—its disruptions, violence, and the shadow of alcohol. Revisiting those words still stirs pain, but it also fosters healing. I've come to understand that I was collateral damage in the war between my parents—a war I neither started nor deserved, but one in which I was unwillingly caught in the crossfire.

Perhaps that's why, as a child, I tried so hard not to take the blame for anything. Deep down, I felt it wasn't my fault, yet I often carried the weight of guilt. With no siblings to deflect responsibility and a household fraught with tension, I internalized the belief that I was the problem—that somehow, I was to blame. Even before birth, I likely absorbed this narrative, listening to the cacophony of screams and confrontations.

One of my most vivid childhood memories is riding in the car and gazing at the homes we passed. I would scrutinize their features, searching for signs of warmth and comfort. At night, the glowing lights within those houses captivated me, sparking dreams of a life where I was wanted and loved—homes brimming with joy and acceptance, everything I felt was missing from my world.

Today, my healing journey has taken a beautiful turn with the arrival of my granddaughter. She is the light of my life, her presence unknowingly aiding in my recovery. In her, I see a child surrounded by love and untouched by the terror or violence I endured. Watching her grow and learn in a positive, loving environment fills me with profound joy.

Though I cannot rewrite the narrative of my upbringing, I can reshape how I view it. From infancy onward, my life has been marked by challenges and abnormal experiences. But these struggles have forged an inner resilience in me—a strength I now see as preparation for a life that demanded adaptability and perseverance. While I haven't always navigated these challenges with grace, I've learned emotional maturity along the way. Today, I choose to see my past not as a burden, but as a testament to my growth and capacity for healing.

While I needed to forgive my parents for their actions, I've found that the most important person in this who needs forgiveness is me. I need to let go of life as I thought it was—WHO I thought I was, and love myself for me, whoever that may be. I am learning more about myself and loving myself more every day. We all need to love ourselves more. Not in a narcissistic way, but in a kind, gentle way, forgiving ourselves for errors and stepping forward to live our best lives.

Janet Hamilton

CEO of The Anomaly Factor
International Life and Health Coach

https://www.linkedin.com/in/janet-hamilton-44054323
https://www.facebook.com/janet.hamilton.148
https://www.instagram.com/Janet10hams
http://www.theanomalyfactor.com
https://www.durhamcombustion.com/

Janet Hamilton is a Life Coach, Intuitive Healer, and Highly Sensitive Empath with 20 years of personal development experience. After a long journey of self-discovery, she has found inner peace and connection, realizing her uniqueness as an anomaly. Once feeling disconnected and burdened, Janet has aligned with her soul's purpose and is now living life to the fullest. Having learned the importance of self-love after years of neglecting herself, she became a self-love guru, breaking through limiting beliefs that held her back. Following a period of burnout and introspection, Janet created a podcast and website to share her insights and help others find their own calm and inner peace. Now residing by a serene lake, she enjoys a balanced life, surrounded by nature and supportive, like-minded individuals. Through her coaching business, Janet empowers others to discover their unique anomalies and embrace their authentic selves.

The Courage to Heal:
My Path from Pain to Personal Power

By Janet Hamilton

Well, hurt, pain, and grief apparently are my best friends. LOL! Little did I really understand just how much till recently.

You see, it started, or so I thought, after completely burning out, taking a bad fall that kept me immobilized for two months, and doing very little for basically two years while I healed. On oh so many levels, little would I realize what was ahead of me. LOL!

Now, just before the burnout happened, I had been looking after my cousin in 2009 and once he moved back home, I started looking after my father, who clearly had the onset of dementia and Alzheimer's, which was in 2010 and a couple of years later, I started looking after my mom who had COPD. My mom also needed assistance helping my grandmother, as her eyesight was not good enough to drive any longer. My parents were divorced and living in different cities, which meant I spent a lot of time on the road, basically living in the car and in multiple doctor's office appointments. I was in overdrive until basically 2024. All the while trying to run our businesses, sell our home, build our new home on the lake, as well as trying to have a life of my own, etc.

Then, in April of 2019, I was on the way to my father's new residence at the Long-Term Care Facility for a care plan meeting, which was previously scheduled when my tire went flat. I am on my hands and knees inflating my tire up to make it to the meeting on time when my phone rings. I answered it, and the woman on the other end of the line (is that even a saying now, considering there are no lines with cell phones?). Anyway, she told me her name and that she was the nurse looking after my mom. She wanted to know if anyone had called me, to which I answered, "Not till now, why?" She told me that

I should get to the hospital as soon as possible, as my mom was losing consciousness. I told her my situation and that I would get there as soon as possible, but obviously had to deal with the tire and dad, as he was still living. I knew I wasn't going to get there in time and would end up rushing to get there, and I was already exhausted. I called the LTC home and told them the situation, and they allowed the appointment to be rescheduled for the next month. That's a whole other story.

I now must deal with getting my tire fixed before I can hit the highway to get to the hospital to be with my mom before she passes. I was lucky enough to find a gas station within walking distance and literally poured my eyes out to the poor, bloody mechanic and begged him to help me so I could go and be with my mom, who was passing. I was exhausted, tired, and in shock. He was very nice, extremely understanding, and kind, and he fixed my tire right away, and off I went to be with my mom. That is only a portion of my typical day.

So, I am calling everyone on the way to let them know if they want to come and say goodbye and be with Mom. I called my brother and sister, my two kids, my sister's kids, and my cousin, who is like a sister to me.

I continued with life, planning my mom's funeral, etc., and between and March 2022, which is when my father passed, I had two aunts that passed away in a Long-Term Facility during COVID-19 and an uncle and my poor, wee Milo, my little ten pound Shi Poo. I had to put Milo down two weeks before Dad passed.

Also, during these two years, I kept moving forward as I had to panic and rush to get my mom's home emptied. She was a hoarder who lived with my grandmother, and I was helping my mom look after her. My grandmother was in her 90s and declining as well; my mom could no longer drive due to her eyesight, which left me doing the driving to her appointments as well. The house needed a lot of work done to get it ready to sell. This was all done at the beginning of

COVID-19, and when the government was starting to announce all the shutdowns. I had to think quickly and figure out what had to be purchased for us to complete the renovations and sell the house for the estate to settle before everything was locked down. Then, on top of all that, trying to navigate our system to protect both of my parents while they were aging, with a lot of health issues, whilst advocating for people in their situation when at the time, there was no help and or assistance when required to either help the individual they were caring for, nor for themselves! Caregivers have little or next to nothing when even looking after their own needs; they become depleted, which is often part of their nature, and there are reasons for this, which, basically, is the law of cause and effect.

I have neglected myself so much, since then, my businesses that my husband and started together in 1997, which was built together around his skill set of being an Instrument Technician, called Durham Combustion Limited and Durham Controls Ltd., my family, myself, etc. and have been trying to get through all the paperwork and playing catch up with my life ever since. My health has been compromised because I unknowingly crossed the line, which is exactly what burnout is.

So, while I was lying around all the time, healing and slowly starting to feel like myself again, I decided to jump into five courses all at once thinking I had so much time on my hands now that everyone has gone, to start figuring out what I was going to do with the rest of my life now that everyone has gone. I started focusing on myself for the first time in my life. I am not dead yet, so what am I going to do with the rest of my life?

These courses, I love; these people are my people, this is where I belong. I have spent 20 years doing personal development and continue to surprise and shock myself at how far I have come. I have finally found real people, who are transparent, honest, real human beings, wanting to connect intimately, without being defensive, without being reactionary, that have compassion, understanding, as well as love for themselves and others. This is not something that was ever taught or modeled to me in my family of origin. So, I sought out these authentic beings who, like me, want to change their lives and change the world.

It is here that I did just that, changed my world, that is. I looked deep inside; I looked back at least four generations in an attempt to unfuck myself. Apparently, I have been living with Chronic Post-Traumatic Stress Disorder, my whole life, thus far. I have unknowingly suppressed my emotions my whole life based on what happened to me and what didn't happen to me, because my mother was so depressed, she was not able to process and be with her own emotional needs, as they were not modeled for her either. I did not get the nursing, I was pablum fed, to shut me up, whether I was hungry or not, I was not held, nor did I get the mirroring that is required.

After my learning and looking back at my journey in life thus far, it is exactly like Steve Jobs stated, "it all makes sense in hindsight when you connect the dots backwards."

They say that frequency and vibration are what you attract, like attracts like, and that it is true—feeling is the secret. However, when trauma is involved, it is much harder to be present and allow the flow of energy that resides inside of us to do what it is meant to do, which is to manifest your heart's desires. Trauma is fast and blocks this energy flow, which is our life's force, our soul. Trauma is not what is done to us, but what happens inside us as a result; we are not what was done to us. For myself, so much happened in the first year of my life and in utero, that it is a visceral feeling in my whole body. It is not safe inside my body to just simply be, until recently and with much love, courage, bravery, and listening to my soul, I started digging, being still, journaling, and being present with myself to slow down my system, reduce my cortisol, which is a huge mitigating factor for health and work on my Parasympathetic Nervous System. Dysregulation in the body causes so many health problems, which end up causing disease in the body, resulting in a disease of one sort or another. Since my traumas happened in the first year of my life, there were developmental and structural areas of my brain that were impaired in development. I get overwhelmed by not only my own feelings but those feelings of others, and I identify and resonate with everyone's pain. I feel like it has given me gifts that I don't yet understand. I had to implement boundaries and choose me for the first time in my life. I was never taught to love myself. I loved everyone but myself. As mothers, daughters, and sisters, we are taught to be the caregivers and look after everyone else but ourselves, which I was doing until I could barely look after myself. It's like the oxygen mask on the plane; we have to put it on ourselves first before we can help others. It was selfish to put myself first, and I have since learned that by not doing just that, I was recreating the same neglect I had endured in my infancy, only this time I was doing it to myself—self-neglect and self-abandonment. All of this energy and or activity that resides in our body and that is not released is resistance to something in our lives that we are fearful of confronting, and honestly, what we resist persists. I had to choose me, put myself first, and turn my back on my family until I heal and allow them to journey on their own path for a bit.

I continued to do the courses, listen to the videos, do the tests, do the self-inquiry, do the competencies, do the videos all to become consciously aware of our own internal traits, what makes us tick, what are our triggers, do we respond or react, so that we can become grounded in our own being, knowing what belongs to ourselves and what belongs to the other. If we can not be a compassionate, abiding presence, holding space for another in need, who are we as human beings?

Deep inside of my being, something was crying to get out, be seen, be heard, be known, be validated, and so on. I have since learned and come to realize that it was my soul, yearning to get out and be the person I was meant to be; only, of course, after a ton of introspection and awareness, aligning with my true passion and purpose. I spent 58 years becoming who the world, my parents, teachers, bosses, friends, etc., made me to be, and now, after aligning and connecting to myself, my oneness, my light, for the first time in my life, I am free! I have had so much more pain and grief to digest and process. I grieved my old self, for she did not know what she did not know, until she knew it. I grieved my old self, and the loss of my potentiality, along with all my loved ones.

Funny enough, I have lived my whole entire life, feeling alone, and abnormal, surrounded by a large family and loads of friends, and now I feel less alone and more connected than ever.

Then, just a few months ago, in February, one of my best friends passed away, and my mother-in-law passed away a few days later. We were supposed to leave on vacation and had to reschedule the vacation to Punta Cana so that we could attend my mother-in-law's funeral and unfortunately, as most things in my life, I was distraught that I couldn't attend my friend's funeral because it was on the same day as my mother-in-law's was and they were in different cities, four hours apart.

During my healing journey, my new understanding of me, myself, and I, my life, and my world, I have changed absolutely everything about me: my mindset, my beliefs, my thoughts, my behaviours, my perspective, my identity, etc., just to name a few, and they were all an inside job. This is what awareness is: I woke up and took responsibility for my life and totally released the responsibility of everything else in my life; it is not all my responsibility. I have changed my interior and now, I am attracting differently in the outside world, such as like-minded people, new opportunities, and possibilities that are endless; the world really is my oyster. I feel like a kid again, dreaming, believing, hoping, and playing in the sandbox of life, doing what I love, what I want, and with positive, like-minded soul shifters from all over the world, connecting, loving, and supporting each other in our pursuits. We are BEING the RIPPLE!

So, my joy is and always has been of service, helping others to free themselves from their own self-sabotaging behaviours, limiting beliefs, and cyclical existence, and feeling stuck. Only now, I serve myself first, then others: it now all starts with me and as a result of my dedication and commitment to myself, I am now doing what I created and want, to help others realize their own passion and purpose discovering their own unique anomaly within and to know that healing is totally possible, I had to go through the darkness to find and be the light.

I am still working with my husband as we wind down into retirement and now want more fun, less responsibility, and have created a way to connect, to serve, and to surround myself with like-minded people.

I am now a self-employed entrepreneur and owner of the new, "The Anomaly Factor" Podcast and "The Anomaly Factor" website where I help people overcome trauma, childhood emotional neglect, parentification, boundaries, self-love and caregiver burnout, the residual effects of narcissism, grief, pain and post partum depression and pyschosis, so that I can help them to heal and find the same inner peace that I have only recently found at age 58. I just turned 59 this past February and finally feel safe within my body for the first time in my life! Better late than never, so they say. So, basically, I am helping them heal from whatever they need healing from and to help them find the unique anomaly within themselves; this is where their essence, light, oneness, joy, creativity, happiness, passion, and purpose lie; this is total freedom. Freedom from chaos, drama, negativity, disconnection, anger, resentment, grief, depression, perfectionism, obsessive compulsive disorder, workaholism, shame, and judgement, etc. We are all on our own healing journey to connect with our true essence, which is possible; I did it, and I am confident that others can do the same.

Let's put it this way, you know the saying "peeling back the layers of the onion," well, I liken myself to the Largest Spanish Onion in the Guinness World Records. I had so many layers, so many Defense mechanisms, so many limiting beliefs, that kept me stuck, and guess what, most of it wasn't even my own shit. Don't get me wrong, I played a huge part, too.

I have overcome so much by listening to my soul, which, by the way, has been crying to get out my whole life, from deep within the core of my being. This has made me extremely resilient and unstoppable, and a highly sensitive empath. I have always known I was meant for more. I have wanted more of all my life; in fact, I was told this over and over, "You are too much!" I guess it's better than "You are not enough!", but the impact felt just like that! I have always had the feeling that I wasn't enough, that I was unlovable, unworthy, that I was abnormal, and believe me, my family and those who know me would most likely agree. Why not grasp everything life has to offer?

I have always wanted more: more love, more peace, more understanding, more compassion, more money, more travel, more knowledge, more connection, just more! Hell, why not? You only live once, so why not enjoy the ride?

Go after your dreams, with focused attention, in the right direction, whatever that is for you. This has come to bite me in the ass, multiple times in life, but oh well, I try and I never give up! I always try to take the high road, learn from my choices, and keep moving forward. If not, you are not learning, building muscle, and living; then, you are dying a slow death on so many levels. You see, I did not know what I did not know, until I knew it! For those of you who don't know, this is exactly what awareness is. I have recently learned that I was raised by a depressed mother and a narcissistic father, who both were emotionally unavailable to me. This is called childhood emotional neglect and I survived two or three major traumatic events at six months of age, on top of a lot of neglect, both physical and emotional;

I would later come to learn that this was not intentional, and they, too, suffered with this as they did not get what they could not then give. This has also been a part of my epigenetic and ancestral lineage, which I have also had to process and heal, unbelievable! The ties that bind us, and they do go both ways, once again, unbelievable!

I love to connect and collaborate with both like-minded people who want to change the world by helping others find peace within as that is where it all begins; if we do not love ourselves and find peace within ourselves, then we cannot be present to love another in an authentic, loving, transparent, and relational way.

Spreading LOVE everywhere! That is all there, in my opinion. We were all brought into this world as pure, loving presence, and it is our responsibility to connect within ourselves back to that, before we became who we are to survive. No one is better than another; we are all equals, and our experiences and circumstances are what make us different.

We are all equals, no one is better than another, we are all deserving, we are all worth it, and we are all lovable. I created a safe space within my website for The Anomaly Tribe to share, connect, and collaborate to RISE and ELEVATE their lives in a safe and supportive atmosphere. We are stronger together and in community! You just need to find your tribe! Know that you are not alone and that you are loved.

I hope to help others heal, so that one day, they, too, can find that same joy, happiness, and inner peace we all aspire to have and BE. I hope and pray that we find world peace; it all starts with us. This is what it is to be responsible. We have the responsibility to show the next generation of young men and women that we can do absolutely anything we put our focused attention on, always choose collaboration over competition, and love over fear.

Transparency, accountability, responsibility, and authenticity, and being relational are what will change our thoughts, behaviours, and mindset, so that our leaders do and be better, to serve and to lead with more empathy, understanding, and compassion; if we cannot be expressive and feel heard and safe to do so, then who and how can we trust?

In the end, we all want the same thing: to be loved, to feel lovable, to feel worthy, to feel important, to be seen, and to be heard. Everyone has a story, they are not alone, and when we can get over the shame of what we have endured, which was not our fault, we can move forward with our lives in peace, freedom, joy, and creativity, and with any luck find your own unique anomaly within and somehow find your way to paying it forward in your own way. Love, peace, and presence to each and every one of you!

I can showcase it in my podcast by doing an interview and then on Instagram, Facebook, and LinkedIn, as well as the many groups with which I belong. I want to showcase success stories of people who have had successes based on coming out of whatever adversity and or disadvantages that they have had to overcome by changing their mindset and behaviours.

Dr. Sonya Alise McKinzie

Founder and CEO of ThriveHER Inc

https://www.facebook.com/DrSonyaAliseMcKinzie
https://linktr.ee/thriveherinc
https://www.thriveher.me/

Dr. Sonya Alise McKinzie is a nationally recognized advocate, author, and humanitarian. A proud single mother from Brunswick, Georgia, she has transformed personal adversity into a mission of empowerment and healing. In 2025, she was named American Mother of the Year® by American Mothers, Inc., and in 2019, she was honored as Single Parent of the Year. Dr. McKinzie holds degrees in Business Administration, Business Management, and Human Services Counseling, and received an honorary doctorate in Humanitarianism in 2024 for her tireless advocacy. She is the Founder and Executive Director of ThriveHER Incorporated, a nonprofit supporting survivors of domestic violence. A certified trauma and recovery life coach, she is also a leading voice in the Marsy's Law Movement. As a 19-time published author, Dr. McKinzie's work centers on healing, resilience, and legacy-building, inspiring women to rise from trauma and thrive with purpose.

Finding Forgiveness and Purpose Through Faith

By Dr. Sonya Alise McKinzie

There's something life-changing that happens when we allow God's word to take root in our hearts. When we surrender to His love and guidance, we begin to see the chains of pain, fear, and brokenness fall away. That's what happened to me.

For years, I lived in the shadows of domestic violence—first witnessing it as a child, and later experiencing it firsthand as a woman. The emotional wounds ran deep, and for a long time, I carried the weight of fear, insecurity, and shame. I struggled with my self-worth, my appearance, and my ability to believe that I was worthy of love and peace.

In the mid-90s, I reached a breaking point. I attempted to end my life—twice. But God had other plans. He spared me, not once but twice, because He had a purpose for my life that I couldn't yet see. Years later, after being diagnosed as borderline diabetic and labeled "morbidly obese," I realized how much I had neglected myself—physically, emotionally, and spiritually.

I tried to move forward, but the pain lingered. I rushed into a relationship before I had healed from a painful divorce, and once again found myself in a dark place. But in the middle of that valley, God gave me a miracle: I became pregnant, despite doctors telling me it might never happen. That child—my daughter—became the light that led me out of the darkness.

During my pregnancy, I leaned on God like never before. I journaled, prayed, and immersed myself in scripture. Psalm 23 reminded me that even in the valley of the shadow of death, I was not alone. I was afraid—of motherhood, of finances, of doing it all alone—but God's presence gave me strength.

Three weeks before giving birth, I finished writing my first book, Heaven Rain On Me, and completed my degree. I began to see that my pain had a purpose. My daughter wasn't just a blessing—she was the beginning of my healing and the key to unlocking my calling.

Years later, in 2016, while sitting in church, I heard God speak clearly:

"Sonya, stop running. Use your experience to make a difference. You've endured abuse—now be a voice against it."

That moment changed everything. I realized that my story wasn't just about survival—it was about purpose. I had been through the fire, but I came out refined, not destroyed. And through God's grace, I found the strength to forgive—even those who hurt me deeply.

Forgiveness didn't come easily. It took years of prayer, reflection, and surrender. But before my abuser passed away in prison in 2021, I had already released the anger and pain. Not for him—but for me. Because I refused to let bitterness define my future.

Today, I stand as a woman healed, whole, and walking boldly in my purpose. I am no longer defined by the pain of my past, but by the strength I've gained through it. I speak out against domestic violence, I mentor others who are navigating their own healing journeys, and I continue to grow in faith and resilience. My path has not been easy, but every step has been worth it—because through it all, God never let go of me.

For many years, I carried a deep, burning anger. It was the kind of anger that doesn't just sit quietly in the background—it shapes how you see the world, how you trust others, and how you see yourself. That anger was rooted in the trauma of watching my mother suffer abuse, and later, enduring that same pain in my own life. It felt like a generational curse, a cycle I couldn't escape. I lived with the weight of that trauma for far too long, believing that my pain was permanent and that healing was out of reach.

But healing has a way of finding us when we're ready—when we're willing to face the truth, even when it hurts. Through prayer, reflection, therapy, and the unwavering support of people who loved me, I began to confront the hurt and fear that had shaped so much of my identity. It wasn't a quick fix. It wasn't a straight line. But slowly, I began to reclaim my peace, piece by piece.

One of the most pivotal moments in my healing journey came in 2020, just before the death of my abuser. I made the decision to forgive him. Not because he apologized—he never did. Not because what he did was excusable—it wasn't. I chose to forgive him because I refused to let that pain have power over me any longer. Forgiveness, for me, was not about him. It was about me. It was about choosing freedom over bitterness, peace over resentment, and healing over hatred.

Forgiveness is often misunderstood. People think it means forgetting, excusing, or reconciling. But true forgiveness is none of those things. It's not about pretending the pain didn't happen. It's about acknowledging the pain, honoring your own suffering, and then choosing to release the grip it has on your life. Forgiveness is a radical act of self-love. It's saying, "I deserve to be free."

When I forgave my abuser, I didn't do it to make peace with him—I did it to make peace with myself. I was tired of carrying the burden of anger. I was tired of letting his actions dictate my emotions, my relationships, and my sense of worth. Forgiveness was my way of taking back control. It was my declaration that I am not what happened to me—I am who I chose to become after it.

Letting go of that anger didn't erase the past. It didn't undo the harm. But it allowed me to move forward with strength, clarity, and grace. It allowed me to see myself not as a victim, but as a survivor. As a warrior. As a woman who refused to be broken.

And just as I had to forgive him, I also had to forgive myself. That part was even harder. I had to forgive myself for staying as long as I did.

For not seeing the signs. For not protecting myself sooner. For the shame I carried, even though none of it was my fault. Self-forgiveness is a quiet, painful process. It requires compassion, patience, and a willingness to see yourself through the eyes of grace.

But once I began to forgive myself, I started to see the beauty in my brokenness. I started to understand that my scars were not signs of weakness—they were proof of survival. They were reminders that I had been through the fire and come out stronger. I began to embrace my story, not as something to hide, but as something to share. Because in sharing, I found purpose.

Today, I use my voice to speak out against domestic violence. I mentor women who are walking through the same darkness I once knew. I remind them that they are not alone, that healing is possible, and that their past does not define them. I walk alongside them, not as someone who has all the answers, but as someone who understands the pain and the power of rising above it.

Forgiveness has given me the freedom to live fully. It has opened my heart to love again, to trust again, and to dream again. It has allowed me to build a life rooted in faith, purpose, and authenticity. I no longer live in the shadow of what was—I live in the light of what can be.

To anyone who is struggling with forgiveness, I want you to know this: it's okay to take your time. Forgiveness is not a destination—it's a journey. And it's a journey you take for yourself, not for anyone else. You don't have to wait for an apology. You don't have to wait for justice. You don't have to wait for the pain to disappear. You can choose forgiveness even in the midst of the hurt. And when you do, you'll find that it's not about letting someone else off the hook—it's about setting yourself free.

Forgiveness doesn't mean you forget. It means you remember without reliving. It means you honor your story without being trapped by it.

It means you choose peace, even when you have every reason to stay angry. And that choice—that brave, beautiful choice—is what transforms pain into power.

As I look back on my journey, I see a woman who refused to be defined by her wounds. I see a woman who chose healing over hatred, faith over fear, and forgiveness over fury. I see a woman who is still growing, still learning, and still rising.

And I am proud of her.

Cindy Hartzel

Heart Soul Confidence-Based Horsemanship™
Horsemanship Mentor/Transformational Coach

https://facebook.com/heartsoulconfidencebasedhorsemanship
https://heartsoulhorsemanship.com/

Cindy Hartzell is a passionate horsemanship motivational coach and the founder of Unbridled Freedom, a transformative program designed to help women reconnect with their inner selves through the healing power of horses. With over forty years of experience working with horses, Cindy has dedicated her life to nurturing the bond between women and these magnificent creatures. Her journey began with her own battles for self-worth and inner peace, finding solace in the silent understanding of horses. Through personal trials, including traumatic injuries and the loss of her cherished horse, RC, Cindy discovered the profound resilience that lies within. She now guides others in overcoming obstacles, embracing vulnerability, and thriving against all odds. Her work is a testament to the power of love, connection, and the human spirit's ability to rise, lead, and live fully. Through her story, Cindy inspires others to find their path to healing and self-discovery.

Through the Storm:
Lessons of Love, Healing, and Freedom

By Cindy Hartzel

Lessons of Love, Forgiveness, and Freedom

A lie may feel burdensome, but the truth—when it inevitably emerges—clears a path toward freedom. For me, the truth struck like an unexpected storm, unraveling everything, yet it delivered a clarity and release I hadn't realized I craved. My journey, my healing, and my ability to forgive have been forged in the ruins of revelations that could have shattered me. Instead, they became the bedrock of resilience and unshakable strength on which I rebuilt my life.

A House of Silence

I was born into a house of silence, where the cracks of dysfunction were hidden beneath a meticulously maintained façade. To the outside world, we were the American dream: a tidy family, a nice home, and the picture of suburban perfection. But behind closed doors, a dark cloud loomed over our house. It was a cloud that carried weight—suffocating and ever-present. I was the youngest of three, but even as a small child, I could sense that something wasn't right. I could feel the unspoken words that hung heavy in the air. It wasn't just the words themselves; it was the emotions, the whispers of pain, shame, and secrets too dangerous to say aloud. I felt them all.

In our house, questions were dangerous. Curiosity was a liability. If I ever dared to disobey the unspoken rules or ask the forbidden question, "Why?" The punishment was swift and severe. One memory stands out among the rest. I was five years old, and I had asked a simple question about why something in our family wasn't like it was in other families I had seen. My father's face darkened, and my mother didn't come to my defense. Instead, I found myself in the kitchen, where a bar of soap was scraped against my bottom teeth and shoved into my mouth. I was sent to my room with the bitter taste of humiliation and the sharp sting of fear. Hours later, the soap still lingered, and so did the lesson: silence was survival.

Silence was the thread that held our family together, but it also strangled us. My father's temper ruled the household, and my mother's narcissistic tendencies only deepened the wounds. Some days, I thought she loved me. Other days, her actions told me that my existence was a mistake she regretted. She drilled into me that I was the most responsible person in the house. Whenever something went wrong, it was my fault. This mantra wasn't just said in private—she declared it at social gatherings, cementing the belief in my young mind. As I grew older, I began to internalize her words. No matter what I did or tried, it was never good enough. I began to believe that I was fundamentally flawed.

The First Cracks

By the time I reached my teenage years, I was painfully aware that our home was not normal. My friends seemed to have the freedom to speak their minds, to explore their independence without fear of retribution. I longed to do the same, but the fear of consequences kept me trapped. I tried—awkwardly, clumsily—to assert myself, but each attempt only reinforced how out of place I felt. My peers didn't understand me, and many chose to keep their distance. Their rejection stung, but I found solace in Skajit, my Welsh pony, and my cat, who understood me in ways humans never could.

As I grew older, the need for control in our household became suffocating. My father tightened his grip, shaming and intimidating me whenever I dared to challenge him. At one point, I was placed on restriction for three months for nothing more than spending time with my boyfriend. The punishment was severe, designed to break my spirit and remind me of who held the power.

Then, at age fourteen, the storm broke. The carefully constructed façade of our family's perfection began to crumble under the weight of long-buried secrets. I learned that my father was not my biological father, that my parents had both been married before, and that I had an older sibling I'd never known. My other siblings had always known these truths, but I had been shielded from them. The discovery was devastating. The life I thought I'd known had been built on lies. The dark cloud that had always haunted our house finally made sense.

A Memory That Shaped Me

Even before the revelation, there had been another, darker shadow that loomed over my childhood. We were raised in a household where both parents worked, so we had a babysitter. I have fond memories of the warmth and safety I felt in her home, a stark contrast to the tension of my own. At her house, we were allowed to be kids: playing, running, swimming, and most of all, asking all the questions we wanted.

But there was another side to those memories, one that I buried deep for years. One of the babysitter's teenage children, a boy much older and larger than I, began to prey on me. At the age of five, I was lured into an office in the garage when no one else was home, and he raped me. I froze, the fear of punishment from my father ringing in my ears. "Children are to be seen and not heard," his voice echoed in my mind. I wanted to scream, to fight, to run, but all I could think of was the beating I would surely face if I made a scene. The abuse continued several times a week for four years.

The physical abuse at home eventually subsided as I entered my teen years, but the scars of the sexual abuse remained. The mental and emotional control in our household replaced the physical violence. My freedom was restricted, my every move monitored.

It wasn't until years later that I began to understand the lasting trauma of those experiences. The pain of my mother's indifference, the weight of my father's dominance, and the violation I endured as a child shaped the core beliefs I carried into adulthood. Yet, even in those darkest moments, a flicker of light persisted—a whisper that told me healing was possible if only I could find the courage to face my pain.

Healing Through Horses

When we moved to a new town, that flicker of light within me grew brighter. It came in the form of a small horse stable, tucked away just up the road from our house. This stable quickly became my sanctuary, a place where I could escape and simply be. It was here that I met Skajit, the Welsh pony who would forever change my life.

Skajit was more than just an animal; he was a companion, a confidant, and a mirror reflecting the parts of myself I had long suppressed. With Skajit, I found a sense of freedom I had never known. Together, we wandered tree-lined trails, exploring the foothills and escaping the confines of a home that often felt more like a prison. Skajit loved me unconditionally, and for the first time, I began to understand what it meant to feel safe and valued simply for being myself.

Skajit's lessons extended far beyond the practicalities of riding. He taught me about trust and boundaries—lessons I had never been allowed to learn in my human relationships. If I pushed him too hard or ignored his cues, he would let me know, whether by refusing to move or offering a gentle nip to get my attention. And yet, no matter how many mistakes I made, Skajit always forgave me, offering me a fresh start each time I returned to him.

This pony became my first true teacher in forgiveness. Through him, I learned that forgiveness wasn't about excusing harm or forgetting past wounds—it was about creating space for healing and growth. It was about letting go of the anger and resentment that weighed me down, allowing me to move forward with a lighter heart.

Skajit's love and wisdom planted the seeds of healing within me. Those seeds would continue to grow and shape me as I navigated the complexities of adulthood, serving as a constant reminder of the lessons he had taught me: the power of trust, the importance of boundaries, and the profound gift of forgiveness.

RC: A Teacher and a Mirror

Years later, another horse entered my life, carrying with him lessons that I needed at that particular stage of my journey. RC was a wild yearling palomino, rescued from uncertain circumstances. From the very moment I met him, I felt a connection unlike anything I had ever experienced before.

RC was more than just a horse—he was a teacher, a mirror revealing my inner strengths and truths. He challenged me to grow in ways I never imagined, pushing me to confront parts of myself that had long been buried. Over the course of a decade, RC and I built a bond rooted in trust and mutual respect.

But our relationship was not without its challenges. In forty years of working with horses, I had only been seriously injured three times— and all three incidents involved RC. These were not mere accidents or unfortunate mishaps. They were pivotal moments that forced me to confront the unresolved pain and fear I carried deep within me.

One of these accidents left me with a triple brain bleed, a stark and painful reminder of the risks inherent in working with animals as powerful as horses. Another incident cost me a finger, shaking the foundation of my trust—not just in RC, but in myself. This second injury left me reeling, overwhelmed by the pain and mistrust that had taken root in my heart.

In the aftermath, I withdrew from RC, unable to face the emotional weight of what had happened. It was during this time of separation that I uncovered one of the greatest truths about forgiveness: it is not a gift you give to someone else but a gift you give to yourself. By avoiding RC, I was also avoiding the parts of myself that needed healing.

To move forward, I had to confront the shame, anger, and fear that had built up over a lifetime. It was only by facing these emotions head-on that I could begin to rebuild the connection we had once shared. In the process, I came to understand that RC was not just a reflection of my journey—he was an integral part of it, challenging me to grow, forgive, and heal in ways I had never before considered.

Leaning Into the Pain

Healing is rarely a comfortable process, and forgiveness is no exception. It requires us to lean into the pain we've worked so hard to avoid, to sit with our discomfort and allow it to teach us. For me, this meant confronting the ways in which my childhood traumas had shaped my beliefs about myself and the world around me.

For years, I had carried the belief that I was unworthy, that my value was tied solely to how well I could meet the expectations of others. These deeply ingrained beliefs kept me trapped in a cycle of fear and self-doubt, unable to fully embrace the life I wanted to create. They were like invisible chains, holding me back from the freedom and joy I longed for.

But as I worked to heal my relationship with RC, those beliefs began to unravel. I started to see them for what they truly were: stories I had been told, not truths I was bound to live by. RC became my guide through this transformative process.

He mirrored my emotions, reflecting back the fear and mistrust I carried within me. When I was hesitant or uncertain, he responded in kind, forcing me to recognize and confront those feelings head-on. Yet, RC also showed me something deeper—the power of resilience. He taught me what it meant to face challenges with courage and to emerge stronger on the other side.

Through RC, I came to understand that forgiveness is not about erasing the past or pretending the pain didn't exist. It's about transforming that pain into something that empowers us, something that allows us to grow and move forward. Forgiveness became not just a way to heal my relationship with RC, but a way to heal my relationship with myself.

The Legacy of Forgiveness

In August 2021, I faced one of the hardest moments of my life: saying goodbye to RC. At just thirteen years old, he was taken from me by a brain stem lesion that left him disoriented and confused. Watching him slip away was heartbreaking, a pain that words can hardly capture. Yet, even in this moment of loss, RC reminded me of the lessons he had always taught—the importance of living fully in the present and cherishing the connections that shape our lives.

RC's passing marked the end of one chapter, but his legacy continues to live on in the work I do today. As I help women and their horses build trust, confidence, and connection, I see the ripple effects of the lessons RC instilled in me. Every retreat, every clinic, and every transformative moment between a horse and its rider is a testament to his enduring wisdom.

Forgiveness, as RC taught me, is not just an act but a legacy we carry forward. It is a gift that frees us from the chains of the past, allowing us to step boldly into the possibilities of the future. Forgiveness is a journey of rediscovering our own worthiness, of reclaiming our power, and of stepping into the light that remains when the darkness fades.

Though RC is no longer by my side, his spirit continues to guide me. His lessons of trust, resilience, and love ripple outward, shaping not only my own life but the lives of others. In this way, his legacy endures, a beacon of hope and transformation that reminds us all of the power of healing, connection, and forgiveness.

The Depth of Forgiveness

Healing is rarely a linear process, and forgiveness is no exception. For years, I carried the heavy weight of anger and resentment toward my parents, particularly my mother. Her rejection when I confronted her about the truth of my origins was a devastating blow. "Consider me dead to you," she said—words that severed any remaining hope of reconciliation.

But I came to realize that forgiveness wasn't for her sake; it was for mine. Forgiveness was about letting go of the power their actions had over me, about freeing myself from the bitterness that had held me captive. It was about reclaiming my life and rediscovering who I was without the burden of unresolved pain.

Through my work with RC and the profound lessons he taught me, I began to understand the importance of releasing the past. Forgiveness didn't mean excusing the harm that had been done to me or pretending it hadn't happened. It meant freeing myself from the pain and shame that had defined my life for so long.

This journey of forgiveness became a journey of rediscovery. As I released the weight of the past, I began to find my voice and my strength. RC showed me that letting go wasn't a sign of weakness but a testament to resilience and courage. In embracing forgiveness, I was finally able to reclaim my story and step into a future that felt lighter and more hopeful.

Living in the Light

Today, I stand in the light of freedom, unburdened by the weight of the past. Forgiveness has given me the courage to release the pain and shame that once defined me. It has allowed me to reclaim my power and embrace the life I was always meant to live.

In the love of my husband, my children, and my grandchildren, I have found the family I always longed for. They have become my anchor, reminding me that love and connection can heal even the deepest wounds. And in the presence of my horses, I have found a sanctuary— a place where I can be my most authentic self, free from judgment and full of purpose.

This is my legacy of forgiveness: turning pain into purpose and transforming the darkest moments into light. Through the love and wisdom of horses, I found my way back to myself. They became my guides, showing me the strength I didn't know I had and the resilience to move forward.

And through forgiveness, I discovered the power to help others do the same. In the light of freedom, we find the strength to heal, the courage to love, and the power to create a life filled with meaning and joy.

Marika Wessels

Founder of Speak Up Queen ~ Voices of Courage

https://www.facebook.com/groups/speak.up.queens
https://www.instagram.com/marikawessels/
https://open.spotify.com/show/4EzmwgJhF9hyi0XSezkwKG?si=zw
IPAP77S4WcPQPSlkodgQ
https://www.marikawessels.com

Marika Wessels is a dedicated advocate and the visionary behind "Speak Up Queen ~ Voices of Courage," a nurturing platform designed to empower women who have transcended their silenced pasts to become unstoppable forces of nature. With a personal history marked by overcoming abuse and adversity, Marika has committed herself to creating a safe haven for healing and growth. Her innovative CORE framework—Courage, Overcome, Responsibility, Enjoy—equips women with the essential tools to break free from their chains of trauma and reclaim their voices. Marika's mission is deeply rooted in the belief that every woman has the potential to rise above her circumstances and achieve greatness. Through Speak Up Queen ~ Voices of Courage, she fosters an environment where once-silenced women thrive as bold, fearless leaders, transforming their painful histories into powerful testimonies of resilience and strength.

Once Silenced Now Unstoppable

By Marika Wessels

To My Loving Husband

My friend, my anchor,

The man who showed up when I needed him the most.
Thank you for loving me when I thought I was broken.
Thank you for showing me what a real man truly is.
Thank you for embracing me—flaws and all.
Thank you for the gift of motherhood, safety, and love.
Thank you for never giving up on me and for your unwavering patience.
I love you—forever and always.

To My Beautiful Son

The light that entered my life and helped me find my way out of the darkness.

Thank you for loving me unconditionally, even when I was learning to love myself.
Thank you for being my mirror, teacher, and greatest motivation.
Your laughter, your hugs, your words— "Mum, just breathe"—have saved me more times than you know.
You are why I keep showing up, healing, and choosing softness over survival.
Because of you, I now know what it feels like to be safe, seen, and truly loved.
You prove that healing is possible—and that legacies can be rewritten.

The Silence That Shaped Me

From a young age, I was loud, bold, and protective. I used my voice to stand up for my sisters and what I believed was right. But the world showed me how unsafe that could be. My voice was taken through trauma, rejection, and neglect. At twelve, I was handed alcohol and cigarettes instead of comfort. No one asked why I acted out—just that I was too much.

Reflecting on those early years, I recall the vibrant energy I possessed—a fire within that compelled me to shield my younger sisters from the harshness of our environment. I remember one particular day when a boy teased my sister relentlessly. Without hesitation, I stepped in, my words sharp and unwavering. At that moment, I felt powerful, a guardian in pigtails.

However, the world around me was not kind to outspoken girls. My assertiveness was met with scorn. Teachers labelled me disruptive, and family members sighed in exasperation. The message was clear: my voice was a problem. The turning point came at twelve when, instead of celebrating my transition into adolescence with guidance and love, I was handed a six-pack of beer and a pack of cigarettes. It was a jarring initiation into a world where my innocence was overlooked, and my well-being was disregarded.

I remember sitting on the cold concrete steps of our back porch, the bitter taste of beer on my lips, the acrid smoke burning my throat. I wanted to scream, to ask why no one saw me, why no one cared. But I swallowed my words, numbing myself with each sip and drag. My actions were cries for help, but they were misinterpreted. Instead of concern, I was met with reprimands. "Why can't you just behave?" they'd say. No one paused to ask what was wrong, to delve beneath the surface of my rebellion.

The Wounds That Weren't Mine to Carry

I was a child forced into adulthood, carrying burdens I didn't create. I tried to fix the chaos around me, believing that if I were just better or quieter, maybe the pain would stop. Attention became a substitute for love. And eventually, I blamed myself for everything. The most complicated person I had to forgive? Was me.

Growing up, our household was a battlefield of unspoken tensions and volatile outbursts. I became the mediator, the peacemaker, constantly navigating the minefield of adult emotions. I remember nights when I'd tiptoe into the living room, finding my mother in tears. I'd sit beside her, a small hand on her shoulder, whispering assurances far beyond my years. "It'll be okay, Mom," I'd say, though I barely understood the weight of her sorrows.

Seeking solace, I turned to relationships that mirrored the dysfunction I knew. I mistook possessiveness for affection and volatility for passion. Each heartbreak reinforced the belief that I was unworthy, that I was the common denominator in my failed attempts at love.

The realisation that I was carrying wounds inflicted by others was both liberating and devastating. I had to confront the narratives I'd built around my worth to sift through the layers of guilt and shame that weren't mine to bear. Forgiving myself became a daily practice, a conscious decision to release the burdens of my past and step into a future where I defined my value.

The Day I Found My Voice

At 17, the weight of my experiences became unbearable. The nightmares, the flashbacks, the constant state of hyper-vigilance—it all culminated in a desperate need to unburden myself. Summoning every ounce of courage, I walked into the local Social Worker's Office, my heart pounding like a war drum.

The detective assigned to my case was a middle-aged man with kind eyes. As I recounted my story, his gaze never wavered, his attention unwavering. When I finished, he leaned forward and said, "I'm proud of you. You've just broken the generational curse." His words were a balm to my wounded soul, though their full significance eluded me then.

His support made me believe that justice and healing were within reach. However, the euphoria was short-lived. Soon after, another detective told me, "You asked for it. No one will believe you." And just like that, the silence returned, and my healing was paused.

The betrayal cut deep. I retreated inward, questioning the validity of my experiences and doubting my perceptions. The courage I'd mustered seemed futile, and I resigned myself to the belief that the disbelief of others would always drown out my voice.

The Awakening

Years later, I found myself again—through my son, my choices, and the life I was building. I started to see that my story wasn't just about pain. I began writing a new chapter, not just for me but for the legacy of my last name. Healing wasn't neat or linear, but it gave me freedom I never knew I needed.

Motherhood was a mirror, reflecting my best and worst parts. Holding my son for the first time, I was overwhelmed by a fierce, protective love—a love I yearned for in my childhood. His innocent eyes held no judgment, only trust and adoration.

As he grew, so did my self-awareness. I recognised patterns in my parenting, echoes of my past threatening to seep into the present. The impatience and moments of emotional distance were remnants of the wounds I'd yet to heal. Determined, I sought therapy, delving into the depths of my trauma, unearthing buried pain, and confronting it head-on.

Writing became both catharsis and revelation. Pouring my experiences onto paper, I wove pain, resilience, and hope narratives. Each word was a stitch, mending the fabric of my identity. I realised that my story held power—not just to heal myself but to inspire others. The legacy of my name transformed from one of suffering to one of strength and redemption.

My 30th Birthday Breakthrough

On my 30th birthday, sitting in a South African airport, I had a conversation with my inner child. I told her, *"Marika, it's time to go."* That moment was sacred. I didn't abandon her—I freed her. I left behind a life of survival and stepped into the unknown to finally discover who I was meant to be.

That day was more than just a birthday. It was a reckoning.

Airports have always been emotional spaces—thresholds between who I was and who I could become. But on this particular day, I was splitting myself in two. I sat with my husband and son, waiting for our flight to Australia, carrying decades of trauma in my chest. The weight of everything I had endured, everything I had kept silent, clung to me like a second skin.

And then it happened. I closed my eyes, and I saw her—my inner child. Marika. Scared. Small. But still holding on.

I whispered to her, in my mind and heart, *"You don't have to protect us anymore. You don't have to be the strong one. It's time for me to take over now."*

Tears streamed down my face—not out of sadness, but relief. I wasn't leaving her behind in shame. I was releasing her from the job she was never meant to carry. I was telling her, *"Thank you. You kept us alive. But now, I want to learn how to live."*

That flight wasn't just the beginning of a new chapter. It was the beginning of my true self.

The Move That Changed Everything

Moving to Australia was more than a relocation—it was a spiritual shift. I finally had the space to hear my thoughts. I started learning about healing, trauma, and art, and I've found a community, starting the real work of healing. I discovered that the people who hurt me were often victims themselves. That didn't excuse them, but it helped me begin the journey of forgiveness.

Arriving in Australia was like stepping into a breath I didn't know I had been holding. Everything felt unfamiliar—new streets, new accents, new rhythms—but within that unfamiliarity was a strange sense of peace. For the first time, I wasn't constantly looking over my shoulder. I could just be.

I also started learning about generational trauma. How pain gets passed down like heirlooms. And as I listened to stories from others—some with different cultures, some with different pasts—I realised I wasn't alone. We were all just trying to unlearn the lies we were told about ourselves.

Understanding that "hurt people hurt people" was not a justification, but it *was* a key. It helped me start unlocking the tightly shut doors inside me. Forgiveness became not just possible but necessary.

Forgiving the Unforgivable

Forgiveness came in layers. For the friends who lied. For the adults who looked away. For the family who didn't understand. I chose to stop rehearsing my pain and start writing my power. I chose peace—not because they deserved it, but because *I* did.

I used to think forgiveness was a performance. Say the words, smile, and move on. But true forgiveness? It cracked me open.

Forgiving friends who betrayed me was a grief I didn't expect. We often talk about breakups in romantic terms, but no one tells you how deeply friendship betrayals can cut. People I confided in twisted my words. People I trusted disappeared when I needed them most. At first, I built walls. However, I eventually learned to build boundaries instead.

Then, there were the adults. The ones who saw the bruises, heard the shouting, sensed something wasn't right—and did nothing. Some of them are still in my life in distant ways. Some I've chosen to never speak to again. But I've made peace with that. I no longer need their apologies to move forward. I've apologized to *myself* for waiting so long.

Choosing peace doesn't mean forgetting. It means giving my soul space to breathe again.

My Mother's Voice

My mother's silence was one of my earliest heartbreaks. I often wondered why she didn't fight harder for me. Why didn't she stop the chaos, the yelling, the pain? It felt like abandonment, even while she was still physically there.

Then one day, over tea and too much unsaid history between us, she told me about her own childhood. About the abuse. The neglect. The fear. She spoke of things I had never heard her say, and I saw her differently.

She wasn't just my mother. She was someone else's broken little girl.

That conversation didn't suddenly fix everything. We still have our gaps. But that moment was the first time I allowed myself to see her through the eyes of compassion, not just as my mother but as a woman with wounds of her own.

Forgiving her meant softening—not my boundaries, but my heart.

The People I Let Go

There's a quiet grief that comes with letting go of people you once loved—family, friends, even partners. I tried, for years, to make it work. To be enough. To be lovable in their eyes. But eventually, I realised that no matter how much I gave, it would never be enough for people committed to misunderstanding me.

Letting go wasn't an act of bitterness—it was an act of liberation.

I began surrounding myself with people who weren't perfect but who were *present*. People who didn't flinch at my story. People who didn't need me to shrink so they could feel tall. That kind of love— mutual, respectful, whole—was new. And it became the foundation for the life I was now building.

Reparenting Myself

Reparenting started as a whisper—something I read about in a book, not fully understanding what it meant. But the more I sat with myself, the more I realised that my healing wasn't just about grieving what I had lost. It was about *giving* myself what I never received.

I began talking to myself differently. Instead of judgment, I offered comfort. When I made a mistake, I no longer said, *"You're so stupid."* I said, *"It's okay, baby girl. You're learning."* I made space for softness. I started taking naps without guilt. I began choosing foods that nourished instead of punished. I let myself cry—not in shame, but in release.

And something incredible happened. The more I mothered myself, the more present I became with my son. I no longer parented from fear, or from reaction—I parented from intention. He didn't just get a better version of me; *I* got a version of motherhood that felt healing for both of us.

From Forgiveness to Freedom

Forgiveness softened everything, especially how I loved and how I let myself be loved. I stopped trying to be a "perfect" wife and mother and started being *present*. My husband saw the change before I even did. He would look at me with such deep patience, holding space in moments where I used to shut down or lash out.

Our 20-second hugs became a family tradition. It sounds silly, but those 20 seconds created a pause, a bridge between overwhelm and safety. When my son wraps his arms around me and says, "Just breathe, Mum," it's not just him comforting me—it's evidence that I've created something different. Something healing.

I started looking in the mirror not to criticize, but to *see*. To honor my stretch marks as stories, my tired eyes as testaments of survival. My reflection became less about flaws and more about *freedom*.

Boundaries and Self-Love

For years, I thought being "good" meant being available to everyone all the time. I said yes when I wanted to say no. I let people cross lines just to avoid conflict. But each time I abandoned myself for someone else's comfort, I felt myself shrinking.

Now, boundaries are my love language—to myself and others. I say no with confidence. I say yes with joy. I don't explain my decisions to people who never took the time to understand my pain. I know that my energy is sacred, and I get to choose how and where it flows.

Self-love isn't all spa days and soft music. Sometimes, it's canceling plans. Sometimes, it's confronting hard truths. Sometimes, it's walking away. And sometimes, it's sitting with myself in silence, no distractions, just breath—and whispering, *"I am enough. Just as I am."*

What Forgiveness Isn't (And What It Is)

People often misunderstand forgiveness. They think it's letting people off the hook. They think it means we're weak. But I've learned that forgiveness is the bravest thing you can do when the world has tried to harden you.

Forgiveness doesn't mean reunion. It doesn't mean trust. It means peace. It means saying, "You no longer get to live rent-free in my mind." It means choosing joy over resentment.

I used to replay conversations in my head, the "what-ifs," the anger, the wish that someone would finally say sorry. But those thoughts held me hostage. When I started releasing them, I noticed my body relax. My breath deepened. My smile returned.

And I realized: forgiveness wasn't a gift for them. It was the gift I had been waiting to give myself.

A Love Letter to My 17-Year-Old Self

Hi Louise,

You were just a girl, trying to survive. Trying to make sense of a world that never made room for your voice. You weren't dramatic. You weren't "too much." You were hurting—and no one stopped long enough to listen.

But I'm listening now.

You did the best you could with what you had. And you held on, even when it felt impossible. You created love out of nothing. You protected others when you needed protection yourself.

I love you for that.

You didn't deserve the shame. You didn't deserve the silence. But today, I reclaim you. I love every version of you—messy, scared, lost, loud, brave.

You are not your trauma. You are your transformation.

The Legacy I'm Leaving

My mission is rooted in truth, in fire, in softness. I want women to know they are not alone. That their pain is real, but it is not the end. That healing isn't just for the lucky—it's for the *brave*. And if no one ever told you this before: You are brave just for surviving.

I've started sharing my story not because I enjoy reliving the pain, but because every time I do, another woman feels less alone. Every time I speak, another voice is freed. Every safe space I create becomes a sanctuary for stories that were once buried.

We are not here just to heal—we are here to *rise*. To lead. To mother. To break curses. To build legacies. And this, right here, is mine.

Love, Marika

#SPEAKUPQUEEN

Once Silenced, Now UNSTOPPABLE

Wendy Firmin-Price

Founder of HEART Equine-Assisted Therapy

https://www.linkedin.com/in/wendyfirminprice/
https://www.facebook.com/wendyfirminprice
https://www.instagram.com/wendyhealingwithhorses/
https://theheartcentreuk.com/
https://www.healingheartsandmindswithhorsescic.org/

Award-winning author, keynote speaker, and Spiritual Awakening Mentor Wendy Firmin-Price fuses sharp psychological skill, 5D intuition with the healing power of horses. As founder of HEART Equine-Assisted Therapeutic Coaching & Therapy, Wendy spent over three decades translating horses' silent wisdom into measurable breakthroughs for leaders, teens, and seekers. A Master Practitioner in Human Change Interventions and multi business owner, Wendy dismantles egoic illusion with fearless honesty, quick wit, and compassion, guiding clients to claim self-worth, cultivate authenticity, and lead from the heart. Her acclaimed books distil spiritual teachings into practical roadmaps that transform relationships, careers, and lives across the world. Whether mud-spattered in a paddock or electrifying conference stages, Wendy speaks fluent horse, human, and higher self, delivering potent "aha" moments that ignite courage, clarity, and sustainable change. She continually proves that when heart and presence unite, extraordinary possibilities become everyday reality— touching individuals, teams, communities, and the planet daily.

A Field of Forgiveness

By Wendy Firmin-Price

I felt the big conker brown bay horse acting jittery underneath me. My mouth was dry, but my palms were sweating through the black leather riding gloves. I couldn't swallow. The energy of the nerves in my stomach wasn't just like a kaleidoscope of butterflies, but more like a swarm of angry wasps.

"You are next!!" bellowed the Adonis-looking instructor. His blonde German looks belied the intolerance of nervous riders.

I was taking jumping lessons to increase my skill and confidence to get over 3'6" jumps, the height needed to pass my horse riding and teaching exams. All well and good, except I was terrified to get over 1'6".

So, there I am, terrified of the jump, terrified of the horse reacting to my nerves, terrified of the wrath of the riding instructor if I dared to wimp out, when I clocked it. That energy, that state of mind, that terror, those feelings of fear permeating every cell of my body. It was the same anxiety I experienced every night, waiting for my alcoholic partner to return home.

What would it be tonight?

What would I be blamed for? Why was he so angry? What would the alcohol bring out in his behaviour this time? How would the violence be taken out on me—another fork stabbing? A knife pulled on me? Or punching me or a hole in the flimsy mobile home walls, where I lived? There was never a way of knowing.

They say every wound has the power to be a womb. Mine came in the shape of that burly bloke, a bottle, and a broken dream. His name was Kevin. He was my partner, the love I once clung to, and the man whose addiction to alcohol became the wild storm that threatened to drown us both.

At first, I played the role perfectly—the fixer, the enabler, the hopeful redeemer. Like most women, I believed if love could save someone, surely mine would. But domestic abuse and addiction don't speak the language of logic. It speaks in lies, silence, slammed doors, and shattered promises. It took a very long time before, slowly and painfully, I realised that I was no longer trying to save him. I had to try and save myself.

The Blame Game

Blame. It's seductive. It gives you a villain and, momentarily, a sense of power. I blamed him for the chaos, the instability, the hollow ache of loneliness that accompanied me to bed night after night—even when he was right there beside me. I blamed him for the constant feeling of walking on emotional eggshells, for the financial disasters, the embarrassment, the shame.

But blame is a poison chalice dressed up as justice. And when I swallowed it whole, it didn't bring peace—it kept me shackled. Horses taught me that. Not through words, but through mirrors. You see, horses don't blame. They respond. They reflect. They reveal. Just like that day in front of the jump, and that was when something shifted.

Have you ever had the "friend" that hands you that self-help book (that, really, they should have read) with the stern command "Here, read this!" 35 years ago, the so-called "new age" was just getting going, so the book by Louise Hay *You Can Heal Your Life* was very revolutionary.

Chapter 1 – You create your own reality. Oh really—what a load of poppycock—if that was true, who would create a reality of debt, domestic abuse, and daily dread?

Chapter 2 – People are your mirrors. You've gotta be kidding me. I am nothing like my alcoholic. I don't cheat, I don't lie, I don't go around hitting people. No, of course, not. And as for the anger and rage, I never got angry. I was Miss Goody Two-Shoes. I threw the book away.

But have you ever heard of the expression by Arthur Schopenhauer, "When truth hits consciousness, first it is ridiculed, then it is violently opposed. Finally, it becomes self-evident."?

You see, even though I threw the book out, I couldn't get out of my head what I had read, ridiculed, and violently opposed! Naturally, I wasn't anything like my alcoholic to the outside world, but I did come to the realisation that maybe he was mirroring how I had cheated and betrayed myself. I was living a lie, pretending all was well in my world with my business, relationship, and well-being. The violence wasn't to other people, but the inward self-attack was far more brutal than any outward alcohol-induced action I was on the receiving end of. Oh, and that avalanche of anger he expressed—I discovered that was the extent of my imploded childhood rage that was being externally projected onto him.

The Choiceless Choice

Have you ever been stuck in a situation, too frightened to stay, too frightened to go? Maybe you know someone caught up in that dilemma. So, when I learnt about creating your reality, you can understand the scepticism I felt. BUT, what if? What if you, I, we could change our thoughts to change our reality? What would that mean for our lives?

So, I dared to. The first place I tried was with my riding. Positive affirmations, visualisations, acting as if. And, yay, it worked—I passed my riding instructor exam; I sailed over those 3'6" jumps (I did fall off in the flatwork part of the exam, but that story is for another time).

And although it wasn't a quick fix, with more and more exposure to spiritual teachers, self-help books, and seminars, I gained the courage to finally stand up to my alcoholic and start taking charge of my life.

What Has All This Got to Do with Forgiveness?

Would you agree that when you have low self-esteem, childhood abandonment wounds, fear of rejection, etc., you are likely to be caught up in people-pleasing, over-giving, and forever forgiving poor behaviour, in order to try and get that validation, love, or approval that is not forthcoming from within.

There are many myths and mistakes made about forgiveness. Let's explore them and see the truth.

1. Forgiveness condones the behaviour. People fear that forgiveness will mean that the person is getting let off. This is not the case. Forgiveness is for your benefit. To let go of the feeling YOU are holding onto.

2. Forgiveness only happens when the other person is prepared to apologise or change their behaviour. If you are going to wait for them to change, then be prepared for a long wait. Forgiveness is for your peace.

3. Forgiveness makes you weak. Yes and no. Forgiveness without future boundaries that are carried through, yes, will make you weak, but in truth, true forgiveness comes from strength.

4. Forgiveness makes them right! The truth is that if you are in a power struggle, non-forgiveness means you have given your power away. They are still in control of you.

5. Forgiveness lets them off the hook. It's an interesting expression, but the truth is that the hook is already in you. Non-forgiveness literally keeps you stuck energetically because they have a hook in you that is siphoning off your energy. Forgiveness actually lets you off their hook literally.

6. It's spiritual/my faith requires me to forgive. Absolutely, it is the right thing, but start with yourself. Spiritual forgiveness does not mean you carry on tolerating poor or dysfunctional behaviour in the name of your belief. Ultimate spiritual forgiveness is recognising that there is nothing to forgive.

This is where I had made the mistake with Kevin. I kept forgiving him because I thought that was the right thing to do, but I never set clear boundaries that I followed through with. And the reality was that Kevin was only ever mirroring the part of me that was punishing myself so harshly. When I eventually learned the power of self-love and self-forgiveness, my life really started to change.

What I didn't know then—but am deeply aware of now—is that forgiveness was never really about him. It was about freedom. Mine. It was about letting go of a story that had worn grooves into my spirit, grooves that kept me riding the same emotional patterns, day after day. The longer I clung to my resentment, the more it fed that internal narrative that said I wasn't safe, wasn't worthy, wasn't enough. And that wasn't just emotional—it had a physical and financial cost. My body carried the tension. My breath stayed shallow. My nervous system was constantly braced for a fall. And my finances were in a mess, too.

Forgiveness was the unbuckling. The unclenching. The permission slip to finally exhale.

The Real Power of Forgiveness

Forgiveness is not about saying it was okay to do what they did—no, it's about releasing yourself from that energetic hook still in YOU. It's about reclaiming the parts of yourself you abandoned while carrying someone else's pain. It's about choosing peace over punishment, and presence over the past.

When you carry resentment, you are essentially carrying someone else's energy in your body, rent-free. That energetic weight causes real symptoms—tension, anxiety, inflammation, fatigue. Forgiveness is the moment you choose to drop that load and say, "No more. I choose me." Non-forgiveness will make you pay the price with illness, relationship problems, finances, and career issues.

The deeper truth? Forgiveness is not fluffy. It's fierce. It's one of the most courageous acts a person can make. Not because it's comfortable, but because it's *clean*. It's uncluttered. It's the spiritual equivalent of mucking out your inner stable. Dirty work, but essential if you're going to walk into a new day without dragging yesterday's manure behind you.

There was a time I thought forgiveness meant being nice. Being passive. Being spiritual. But now I know—it means being powerful. It means standing in the full truth of who you are, acknowledging what happened, and choosing to no longer be defined by it.

Wendyism: "Forgiveness doesn't make them right—it makes you ready and light."

It's a rite of passage. A soul maturation. And every single time I've helped someone cross that inner bridge—from pain to peace, from blame to bravery—whether in a field with horses or in a tearful coaching conversation, I've witnessed transformation.

Forgiveness clears the static between you and your intuition. It sharpens your sense of self. It restores access to your joy. And it unlocks love—the real kind, the unconditional kind, the sustainable kind.

That is the field I live in now. Not just literal fields with my 28 horses, but the energetic field of forgiveness. It's where freedom lives. It's where truth gallops. And it's where I invite others to come, take a breath, drop the armour, and let their hearts be heard.

And it all began the moment I chose to let go—not of what happened—but of the hold it had on me.

Wendyism: Forgiveness isn't forgetting the hurt.
It's remembering your worth.

Effective Blaming

As we discussed earlier, it can be very easy to play the victim. If it wasn't for so and so, I would have been able to do X Y Z. Most people I work with have a parent, partner, or person they want to blame for why their life is not going well. And I believe that may be a state and stage you need to go through. However, when you can discover the TRUE value of that event, you can say, "If it wasn't for ..." and list the positive events that have come about. That is when you discover true power and forgiveness. Remember, everything is either a lesson, an opportunity to grow, or a gift, or all three.

So, what were mine? As my self-esteem grew into self-love, that gave me more confidence to make changes in my own life. I finally overcame the fear that my alcoholic would kill my horses if I left him and had the courage to leave him. I have since been with a wonderful, kind man who later became my husband, and we have been together for over 30 years now.

But here is the real gift of that gruelling time. The spiritual awakening I received from being in that dysfunctional relationship totally transformed not only my life and relationships, but the learnings and self-growth I gained from that period are now transforming lives daily.

So inspired by those early "new age" books, I ended up training to be a Metaphysical Counsellor, Teacher, and Practitioner. Discovering the power of thought, combined with understanding the laws of the Universe and how you can create your reality, became the basis for my work.

But here is where the uniqueness of that first realisation, standing in front of the jump in absolute terror and what it was really mirroring about the fear in my life, gave birth to me being one of the earliest pioneers in equine-assisted therapy in the 1990s. In the beginning, I used to just help other riders terrified of riding, horses, or jumping by discovering what the real fear was in their life.

Then this quickly evolved into working with the horses, even before the person rode them. Now, it is mainly working on the ground with horses combined with my unique HEART therapeutic coaching. Within this evolution, there has been a magical Self-Mastery through the Horses Course. Interestingly, module 9 is all about forgiveness. Working with the horses created powerful lessons. One of the most profound sessions my students had was when we visited a rescue sanctuary.

Ernie's Sacred Stillness

Pretty much all of the horses had either come from a history of being abused, neglected, or abandoned. This particular day, we were working on forgiveness. In the morning, we were learning about the horses' unsavoury backgrounds, which in itself was a challenge. In the afternoon, we were out in the fields where the horses were loose and sent out an energetic request for a horse to come and help us.

The next thing we knew, this HUGE 18hh horse called Ernie of its own free will sauntered over to where the group was. We gathered around him to do a specific forgiveness exercise. Now, when Ernie first joined the sanctuary, he was extremely violent. The abuse he had suffered for growing into such a large horse was horrendous and understandably reached a point where he felt he had to fight back. Consequently, he got labelled dangerous as he put several people in the hospital.

Ernie was patiently introduced to James French's Trust Technique that totally transformed him into a kind, loving horse. We had completed the specific exercise on forgiveness that we did "through" him, and thought we had finished. Meanwhile, still Ernie stood of his own accord in the middle of us all. I received the intuitive guidance to do forgiveness to the farmer who had abused him and also to forgive Ernie for his behaviour (this seemed extremely off to me, but I went with it anyway).

At the end of the exercise, we had the most heart-wrenching, heart-opening, heart-healing experience we had ever had in the HEART equine-assisted therapeutic coaching sessions. We were all surrounded around him a bit like a horseshoe, and without a word of a lie, Ernie looked each student in the eye as if to say thank you. Then Ernie walked off, leaving a pile of students on the floor in awe and gratitude and tears for witnessing such a profound experience.

"If Ernie can totally transform his behaviour and attitude to humans in spite of how he has been treated, what excuse do I have for not forgiving people in my past?" exclaimed one of my dumbstruck students.

So, having the pleasure of working with the horses to help heal humans of their life challenges is just the best feeling. So much so, we have also started a Community Interest Company called Healing Hearts and Minds with Horses, which specialises in transforming the lives of teenagers and their families. By creating a safe environment with the horses, we are able to give anxious teenagers the chance to be seen, be heard, and understood, thus helping them find different ways to get through life rather than self-harming or feeling suicidal or using out-of-control behaviour.

To My Reader

If you are still holding on to rage, heartbreak, betrayal—know this: You are not broken. You are breaking *open*. And there's wisdom in your wounds if you dare to look. Forgiveness won't make the past prettier. But it will make *you* more powerful. Let the pain teach. Let the horses lead. Let the heart rise.

And when you're ready, take the reins back. Get back in the saddle of that relationship, that career, that risk. Your freedom is waiting.

Remember, and I reiterate: Life is always giving you a lesson, opportunity, or gift. Or all three. I am in huge gratitude for my alcoholic, and whilst I wouldn't want to have to go through that all again, I am so thankful for all the lessons in self-love, forgiveness, and life purpose that came about from it. Ironically, it's thanks to him and my journey out of it that have empowered thousands of lives to be transformed and countless lives saved. There is always a real life beyond the hurt.

Wendy Firmin-Price

Dr. Breanna BOSS James

She BOSSIN' Up
Life Strategist & Business Coach

https://www.linkedin.com/in/breannajames/
https://www.facebook.com/msjames637
https://www.instagram.com/bossupmylife
https://linktr.ee/drboss
www.UnleashTheBossWithin.com

Dr. Breanna "BOSS" James is a sought-after expert on women's empowerment, business coaching, and life solutions, who's been featured in multiple magazines and platforms. She started her career over 14 years ago, bringing a wealth of experience in HR, coaching, and training. After overcoming personal struggles like fear, low self-esteem, procrastination, poor credit, and debt, she discovered the path to freedom and transformation, using her journey to inspire and guide others. When she's not helping women redefine themselves and build businesses based on biblical principles through She BOSSIN' Up, or providing life and health insurance and homeownership solutions through P31X, you'll find her studying the Bible, decorating cakes, reading, target shooting, or nurturing her plants. To learn more about Dr. James and how she can help you achieve your goals, visit https://linktr.ee/drboss. Boldly Overcome Struggles and Setbacks as you positively transform yourself Body, Occupation, Soul, and Spirit.

The Battle Within: Overcoming Self-Betrayal and Embracing Forgiveness

By Dr. Breanna BOSS James

I have survived betrayal, rejection, abuse, and abandonment, but the pain of disappointing God and myself again cut deeper and lasted longer than all of them combined. It was me versus me, and I ignored God and His Word in the middle of my internal battle and lost terribly.

The thing is, I knew better. I had been taught principles of stewardship, faith, and obedience. But when it came time to apply them, especially to my finances consistently, I failed terribly. I made impulsive decisions, trusted the wrong voices, and allowed fear and pride to guide me instead of wisdom and the Holy Spirit.

Most of my biggest mistakes weren't made out of intentional rebellion but out of misaligned desire and responsibility. I wanted to succeed for the glory of God, to help others, to grow my business, and to make something out of the opportunities in front of me. There were moments when I could have stopped. Times when the Holy Spirit whispered warnings. Scriptures I read that challenged my choices. But I silenced them with justifications I told myself:

"God wants me to start a business."
"This is a big faith move."
"I deserve this after everything I've been through."

But none of it was rooted in obedience.

The greatest reality was embracing that disobedience, even when dressed up in good intentions, is still rebellion. In my efforts, I neglected His timing, wisdom, and way. My actions revealed that deep down, I didn't believe the Word like I told myself I did. Second, I was trying to compensate for areas of my life that felt empty. I was striving for life and business success at any cost and was failing miserably. I mean nothing I did worked. Everything I diligently pursued failed. The hustle and grind became a way to prove to myself I was okay, that I was in control, that I could create the life I wanted, even if I had to go into debt to do it.

I had a plan and didn't think I was being careless. Yet I indeed was careless because I didn't do or believe better, even though I knew better. My reality was that, as much as I wanted to, I didn't truly buy into and believe the whole Word as pure truth and a means to live by all of its principles fully. If I did, I would have made better, God-inspired decisions. Instead, I took the advice of the world and thought I was making wise decisions by following their lead. I figured they obtained the success and financial status I desired, so why not go along with their instructions?

I invested in programs and services that sounded good, but they weren't from God. I made decisions out of fear of missing out rather than out of faith in what God had for me. I ran my business on emotion and exhaustion instead of wisdom and peace. Every financial choice I made from panic and that place of misalignment took me deeper into a pit.

When I drilled it down, I made money decisions out of fear, desperation, ego, and even pride. I said yes to opportunities I couldn't afford. I avoided budgeting because I was lazy and didn't want to face how short I was. I made investments without waiting in prayer and confirming the decision with the Word. I bought into shiny promises and borrowed to try and fill desperation-laced voids. I was even caught up in giving out of emotion instead of obedience.

Every unconfirmed choice piled onto the next, creating a mountain of grief and overwhelm, I tried to pretend it didn't exist. Don't get me wrong here, I prayed about every situation and every decision. What I neglected to do was *wait* until I heard an answer confirmed by the Word. I just did what I wanted to do and what felt right. This is a huge mistake. Just because something looks good and feels good, doesn't mean it's the goodness of God. The Word warns us, "...Even Satan disguises himself as an angel of light" (2 Corinthians 11:14).

At first, I was okay with paying everything back. I had even put a solid plan in place to pay off all my debts, and I was steadily progressing. However, the unexpected happened: my job assignment was abruptly ended. I thought I would easily transition into another role, but month after month, as I applied to over 300 jobs and received nothing but rejection letters, my hope dwindled. My business still wasn't growing well enough to sustain me, and the steady income I had counted on was gone. The financial pressure became overwhelming, and with no consistent income, my plan to strategically pay off my debts crumbled before my eyes.

What hurt most wasn't the loss of money and debt. It wasn't even the creditor calls or the other great opportunities I had to pass up. Those things indeed hurt, but what cut me to my core was the realization that I was not honoring God with my actions. I caused myself to be a poor witness to His glory and kingdom. My deepest desire is for my life to glorify God, and I was living the exact opposite; in that moment, I was oblivious to that reality. It was all smoke and mirrors. The self-deception of I'm trusting God and waiting on Him, but not trusting and waiting. I didn't trust Him enough to do things His way and in His timing, even after all the Scriptures, sermons, and chances.

Eventually, the consequences came. The bills piled up. The collector calls started. The sense of peace vanished. I found myself in financial ruin, but worse than that, I was spiritually bankrupt. I couldn't pray about it without crying. I couldn't read the Word without feeling shame. I avoided scriptures about money because they reminded me of how I failed. And even when I repented, I still didn't feel free.

It seemed like I was sitting in my mess way longer than others in the same situation. Deep down, a part of me believed God wanted me to suffer for my disobedience and that He'd never redeem me from the consequences of my actions.

Each business failure stung deeper than the last, not just because of the financial loss but because they symbolized a loss of direction and identity. I was drowning in expenses from coaching programs to branding, marketing, and subscriptions. My dreams started to feel more like burdens. My ambition became a snare.

The Guilt That Lingered

It's strange how we can believe God forgives us but still live imprisoned by guilt.

I repented. I cried. I told God I was sorry over and over again. I opened my Bible, studied Proverbs, and quoted scriptures about stewardship and abundance. But something inside of me still whispered, "This won't work for you, you can't be trusted." I started to believe I was broke and broken beyond repair.

The negative self-talk had me subtly bound in a way I can't even describe. I bought into the voice of the enemy telling me:

> "You messed everything up."
> "You're pathetic and worth nothing, completely worthless."
> "You don't do anything right."
> "God might forgive you, but He'll never trust you with His resources again."

I believed those lies for far too long. I was stuck in a downward spiral, and I didn't know how to get out. I would speak one thing out loud and then meditate on the exact opposite. I would cast my cares over to Jesus, and then, in the next few minutes, I would pull them back.

The shame of disobeying God and self-betrayal was brutal. I had harmed myself and my life in a way no one else could. And worse, even though I knew how to come back from it, I struggled with executing the comeback. Even after repentance, I felt spiritually, emotionally, mentally, and financially paralyzed. I believed in God's grace and mercy, but didn't allow them to be extended to myself. I wouldn't accept the gift He desperately wanted to give me, the gift Jesus suffered and died that I might have.

I kept reliving my mistakes, repeatedly rehearsing every wrong in my mind. I kept looking back, wishing I had made different choices, trying to rewrite the past in my thoughts. Of course, that never worked. It only made me feel more defeated, realizing that I could forgive others for anything, but I couldn't figure out how to show myself the same grace and mercy and forgive myself.

But God...

The Point of No Return

The strangest things move me to action or give me clarity. I think back to looking at the neighbor's rose bush. One day, it was full of colorful roses, and the next day, Granny cut all the roses off and cut the stems down low. The once vibrant, flourishing bush looked rough and barren. I stared at the seemingly lifeless bush, and since I didn't know anything about roses, I couldn't understand why she cut them back so much and how in the world they would grow back as vibrant.

The thing with roses and other flowers and bushes of this sort is that when they are deeply pruned and get good sunlight and water, they grow even stronger and more vibrant than before. A couple of months later, I walked outside and looked to the right and saw the most beautiful red and pink roses on top of very tall stems. I was amazed. I hadn't even noticed the stems growing and the roses budding.

Looking at this, my mind went straight to forgiveness and my situation. I've been hurt, cut deep, with serious bruises. It didn't seem like things would get better, or I'd grow and develop in great ways. Yet, even though at one point I felt low and barren, I knew that if I would dig into the Word, pray, trust God, and always forgive myself and others, I would be free to be more vibrant and to live my life in purpose and on purpose. The truth is, forgiveness and repentance open your life to new beginnings without hanging onto the baggage of the past.

It was on this day that things changed. Even though I felt like the Prodigal Son on repeat, returning with nothing, ashamed to ask for help, I did. Sitting there, face and shirt drenched with tears, I finally decided to let go of myself and my way and submitted myself and allowed God to meet me in my brokenness.

I heard God's voice.

He didn't come with condemnation, He came with truth and compassion. Not with a list of all I had done wrong (it was clear I already knew that), but with a reminder of who He is, what He's done, and who I am in Him. He reminded me that, "Therefore if any man be in Christ, he is a new creature: old things are passed away; behold, all things are become new" (2 Corinthians 5:17, KJV). I had read it many times, but this time was different. I received it. I allowed that truth to settle into the deepest part of my guilt and shame.

Then, it felt like a whisper sang directly to the depths of my soul. *"You are not your financial mistakes. You are my child. You have to choose to let all things be new. You have to choose not to keep picking the old back up."*

I cried as I realized that forgiveness wasn't just something to accept from God; it was something I had to extend to myself. Something shifted in that moment. I realized I was waiting to feel forgiven before I accepted that I was. God doesn't operate on feelings. He operates in truth.

That's when my true journey began. I forgave myself and let it go. I cast all those cares over to Jesus and didn't snatch them back.

Why Self-Forgiveness and Letting the Pain of the Past Go Is Necessary

So many of us stay stuck because we haven't released ourselves from the past. We cling to the version of ourselves who messed up, disappointed, and fell short, as if punishing her is the only way to prove we're sorry. Jesus didn't die so we could stay in cycles of guilt, shame, or lack. He died so we could be free, indeed.

Forgiveness, especially self-forgiveness, is not pretending nothing happened. It's acknowledging the truth of the situation and choosing to align yourself with God's truth, rather than succumbing to guilt, shame, and the lies of the enemy. Repentance is vital. It's a doorway to the transformation you desire. Forgiveness is the freedom that allows us to walk through that doorway and into new life. If God doesn't condemn me, who am I to keep condemning myself?

"There is therefore now no condemnation for those who are in Christ Jesus" (Romans 8:1).

The Biblical Process of Forgiveness and Release

Forgiveness is a process. It begins with repentance, an honest turning away from sin and turning toward God (Acts 3:19). But then comes the harder part, releasing. Letting go of what I could not change, the past. Accepting that while I made mistakes, I am not my mistakes. Isaiah 43:18-19 became real, "Forget the former things; do not dwell on the past. See, I am doing a new thing! Now it springs up; do you not perceive it?"

I had to walk this process slowly, prayerfully, and with intentionality. I had to choose to stop replaying every poor decision I made. I had to stop punishing myself with memories. And I had to renew my mind daily (Romans 12:2). Each day, I made declarations over my life:

- I am a wise steward.

- I have the mind of Christ.
- I walk in financial freedom.
- I am not bound by my past.

It didn't happen overnight. Some days, I still felt the sting. But as I replaced lies with truth, things shifted. I began to see myself the way God sees me. I no longer measured my worth by the balance in my account or the number of mistakes on my record. I measured it by the cross. By the price Jesus paid to redeem me.

Redefining Me

The truth is, I am not the same person who made those mistakes. I've grown in my relationship with God, and I'm finally *anchored* in Him, His Word, His grace and mercy, and His truth. Redefining myself according to the Word was the most powerful part of my journey. The world labeled me as irresponsible, reckless, and untrustworthy. But God says I am redeemed (Ephesians 1:7), chosen (1 Peter 2:9), and equipped for every good work (2 Timothy 3:17).

I began to walk differently. I stopped disqualifying myself from opportunities. I no longer chase validation in my pursuit of success in my God-designed purpose. I've learned to pause, pray, plan, pray, wait, and then execute. I ask God and wait for His answer before I give, before I invest, before I spend. And when I mess up, I correct it with courage, grace, and mercy, not condemnation. Now, I teach others what I've learned.

I'm no longer dragging around the weight of the mistakes I made and who I used to be. I'm walking in the freedom of following the wisdom of the Word and who I am now.

Not because I earned it, but because I decided to receive it.

To You, the One Who Still Feels Stuck

If you're reading this and you've been where I was, stuck in the guilt and shame of your mistakes, I want you to know repentance is not about earning God's love. You already have it. It's about returning to alignment with His truth. And forgiveness, especially forgiving yourself, isn't a weakness. It's warfare. It breaks the enemy's grip of guilt and shame and gives you back your voice.

Repent and embrace God's forgiveness. Forgive yourself. Release the weight. Renew your mind. And rise up boldly!

Let go of the guilt. Lay down the shame. Release the version of you who made those negative decisions and embrace the version of you God designed from the very beginning.

You are NOT beyond restoration. You are NOT beyond wisdom. You are NOT beyond redemption. You CAN be trusted again. Because you are who God says you are, you *can* do what He says you can do. And you can have what His Word says you can have.

Remember that nothing, *NOTHING,* can separate you from His love or His plan for your life when you're in Him, Christ Jesus.

A Prayer of Forgiveness, Restoration, and Freedom

Father God,

Thank you for your grace and your mercy. Thank you for loving me even when I've fallen short and made poor choices. I've carried shame, regret, and guilt, and I lay it all at Your feet. I repent for not trusting You, for ignoring Your Word, and for the financial decisions I made outside of Your will. I've mishandled what you entrusted to me; my time, money, decisions, and body.

Lord, help me to receive Your forgiveness. Teach me how to extend that same forgiveness to myself and others. Remind me daily that I am a new creation in Christ. Help me see myself through Your eyes as redeemed, restored, and whole.

I break every agreement I've made with the lies of the enemy that tell me I am unworthy, incapable, or disqualified. I replace those lies with your truth. I am forgiven. I am free. I am called. I am able.

Give me wisdom. Teach me to steward well. Guide my decisions. Strengthen my trust in You and help me walk boldly in the purpose You've designed for me.

I am not my failures or my past. I am your child. And in You, I live, move, and have my being.

In Jesus' name, Amen.

LaShahn Patrice

Founder and CEO of Milestone Life Strategy Institute

https://www.linkedin.com/in/lashahn-taylor-258bba1b0/
https://www.facebook.com/lashahnt
https://www.instagram.com/lashahn
http://www.milestonelifestrategy.com/
https://www.lashahnpatrice.com/

LaShahn Taylor is a woman who has turned pain into purpose and setbacks into stepping stones. A proud Fisk University alumna, she now resides in Metro Atlanta with her loving husband, Dell. As a certified Toastmaster, published author, Professional Life Coach, and global corporate trainer, LaShahn has spent over 30 years helping others rise above life's toughest moments. From building direct sales teams of over 4,000(expanding across 7 countries) to owning the largest female-owned tour bus companies on the East Coast, she's broken barriers with unwavering faith and grit. Committed to community service, she has helped thousands overcome limitations to live fuller lives. Her creative soul shines through her work as a singer, actress, and voice-over artist. Above all, LaShahn is a devoted mother of five and "Gramsuga" to two, her life stands as a living testimony that with forgiveness, healing, hope, and success are always within reach.

Whispers of Worth:
How Affirmations Helped Me Forgive and Heal

By LaShahn Patrice

There was a time in my life when waking up felt like a punishment. Each sunrise was another reminder that I had to survive one more day of heartbreak, disappointment, and despair. I wasn't just living through abuse; I was suffocating in silence, shame, and emotional torment. But somewhere in the cracks of my brokenness, I stumbled upon a lifeline I never expected: affirmations. And through those daily declarations, I found something even more powerful than healing—I found forgiveness.

From Free-Spirited to Shattered

As a corporate trainer, life coach, and professional speaker, people often see the polished version of me—the woman who walks into rooms radiating purpose and passion. But long before the titles and accomplishments, there was a young woman full of dreams and fire, fresh out of college and thriving in Atlanta. Life was a blend of community service, church events, laughter-filled nights, and spontaneous road trips with friends. I was free-spirited, kind, grounded in faith, and full of joy. Back then, everything felt possible.

Then came a man who changed the course of my life. Tall, dark, handsome, with a magnetic presence and a military officer's poise, he captured my heart effortlessly. He was charming and compassionate, a widowed father with three young children. The idea of becoming an "instant mom" scared me, but love—real, consuming love—has a way of rewriting the rules. We built a life together, had two more beautiful children, and shared a home filled with laughter, responsibility, and what felt like purpose.

But love, when taken for granted or twisted by pain, can become a silent prison.

I wish I could tell you the moment things shifted—the exact day he went from my best friend to someone I barely recognized—but trauma doesn't always have a timeline. What began as subtle changes in tone and mood eventually spiraled into full-blown abuse.

The Party That Broke Me

The moment my world truly shattered wasn't in the privacy of our home—it was in public, at a party, surrounded by people I knew.

It started off as a typical evening. I smiled, made small talk, and pretended everything in my world was fine until whispers started to reach my ears. Whispers that turned into a blunt truth: **my husband had fathered a child**—with **my babysitter.** The very woman I trusted to care for my children was now the mother of his secret child. She also worked for him, so this betrayal wasn't just intimate—it was intentional.

I asked him about it. Not in anger. Just... needing truth.

His response? He **jumped on me.** Physically. Violently.

In front of others.

I can't describe the mix of humiliation and pain. Everyone knew about the baby. Everyone except me. I was the punchline of a cruel joke, the last to know about the betrayal that unraveled the seams of my life. My heart didn't just break—it exploded into a thousand pieces. I had never felt so small, so exposed, so unprotected.

And still—I stayed for a while.

Because that's what trauma does, it convinces you that maybe you're the problem. That maybe if you were prettier, smarter, and more agreeable, he wouldn't have done what he did.

That night should've been the end, but instead, it became a turning point.

The War Inside Me

The abuse wasn't just physical. It was emotional, psychological, and spiritual. Words became weapons. He'd call me names so cruel, they lodged themselves in my psyche like barbed wire. And eventually, his voice became mine.

I couldn't look in the mirror without hearing those insults. My thoughts became darker each day.

"You're worthless."

"You'll never be enough."

"No one else will ever want you."

Even when he wasn't in the room, the war raged on—in my own mind. Add in financial instability, and the pressure of five children looking up at me for strength I didn't have, and it's no wonder I spiraled into hopelessness.

I would wake up crying and go to bed the same way. I felt useless. Unlovable. Forgotten.

And somewhere in the darkness, I stopped praying for peace. I started praying for death.

I prayed to die. I begged God to just let me go in my sleep. I couldn't see a way out. I couldn't see **myself** anymore.

That voice—his voice—soon became my own internal dialogue. I was trapped in a marriage where every word cut deep, and every breath felt like a struggle. The betrayal of infidelity, the suffocating financial pressure, and the impossible weight of being strong for five children turned my world into a war zone. And the worst battles were the ones happening in my mind.

The Unlikely Lifeline

Then, serendipity knocked.

A neighbor, seeing the sadness I tried so hard to mask, handed me a book on affirmations. At first, I brushed it off. I had always loved to read, but I didn't have the energy to digest hope. But something about the word "value" in the title drew me in. Maybe it was desperation. Maybe it was a divine intervention. The book had the word "value" in the title, and that one word stopped me cold. I hadn't felt valuable in years.

But I opened that book, and in doing so, I cracked open a door to a new life.

At first, I just read the affirmations. Then, I started to whisper them aloud:

"I am worthy."

"I am strong."

"I am capable."

"I am happy, healthy, wealthy, and wise."

Each phrase felt foreign at first—like trying on a coat that didn't quite fit. But I kept going. I repeated them in the mirror, in the car, in bed. I whispered them through tears. I didn't believe them yet, but I hoped one day I would. With each repetition, I chipped away at the lies I had been fed—and worse, the ones I had come to believe.

Healing, One Word at a Time

Affirmations weren't just positive thinking. They were survival. They were my armor. They were my truth. Those affirmations were seeds. And though my spirit felt like dry, cracked ground, they began to take root. I started walking taller. Smiling without pretending. Dreaming again.

The Turning Point

Consistency changed everything. The more I affirmed my value, the more I saw glimpses of the woman I had once been—ambitious, joyful, radiant. I started walking taller, speaking up, and dreaming again. My self-esteem, once shattered, began to rebuild one affirmation at a time.

I was offered a leadership role with a Fortune 500 company, something I hadn't even dared to pray for. It felt like the universe was finally responding to my whispered truths. Serendipity wasn't just a cute idea; it was my reality. The more I aligned with my worth, the more my world shifted to reflect it. The woman who had once been crushed beneath betrayal and brokenness was being rebuilt. Stronger. Clearer. Radiant.

Affirmations didn't erase the pain. But they gave me the strength to face it head-on. They reminded me that **what happened to me didn't define me.** They gave me permission to forgive—not because he deserved it, but because **I did.**

The Path to Forgiveness

People often ask how I forgave him.

The truth? I didn't wake up one day with a sudden surge of mercy in my heart. Forgiveness came quietly. It came in pieces. It came when I realized that holding onto hate was chaining me to my past just as much as the abuse did.

Forgiveness wasn't about saying what he did was okay.

It was about saying I was no longer going to let his brokenness define my value.

I forgave to be free.

Free from the lies. Free from the shame. Free from the narrative that I was not enough.

Let me be clear—**forgiveness was not easy**. I wrestled with it. I didn't want to let go of the anger. It felt justified. But eventually, I realized the anger was costing me too much.

Forgiveness didn't mean pretending it didn't happen. It meant releasing **his power over my peace.** I chose to forgive so I could move forward without carrying the weight of what he did. I chose to forgive myself, too—for the nights I stayed, the times I believed his lies, the pieces of myself I gave away hoping to earn love.

Forgiveness came as I affirmed my healing, my growth, and my right to joy. And perhaps the most unexpected part? I began to forgive myself, too—for staying so long, for doubting my worth, for believing the lies.

Today, I Rise

Today, I'm no longer the woman who cries herself to sleep.

I am a wife, mother, grandmother, entrepreneur, author, speaker, life coach, and global business builder. More than that—I am whole. I am free. I am loved. I am **me** again.

I didn't get here by chance. I got here through **grit, grace, and growth.**

The journey hasn't been easy, but every affirmation was a step forward. Every whispered truth was a light in the dark. I am proof that no matter how far gone you feel, healing is possible. Forgiveness is possible. And joy—abundant, soul-filling joy—is waiting on the other side.

For You, Sister

If you are reading this and silently breaking or battling your own darkness, I see you!

If you've been betrayed, beaten down, or forgotten, please hear me: **You are not alone.**

There is a path back to you. It may be slow. It may be messy. But it is possible.

Say it even if you don't believe it yet.

"I am worthy."

Say it again.

Let those words plant roots in your soul. Let it begin to echo louder than the lies.

Because you are worthy! You always have been.

What you are looking for is looking for you—and it starts with believing in your right to be whole, happy, and free.

Reflection: Your Journey to Forgiveness

Before you close this chapter, take a moment to reflect—not just on my story, but on your own.

Ask yourself gently and honestly:

- Have I been carrying, hiding, or suppressing pain that I need to work through?
- What lies have I believed about myself because of someone else's actions?
- Who or what do I need to forgive to be free?
- Have I unintentionally been punishing myself for someone else's betrayal?
- What would it look like to start treating myself with love, grace, and kindness?
- Am I willing to believe I am worthy of peace, healing, and joy?
- What would my life feel like if I truly let go?

Forgiveness doesn't mean forgetting or excusing harm. It means **choosing freedom**. Freedom from the pain. Freedom from bitterness. Freedom to breathe again, love again, live again.

Journal + Affirmation Prompts: Speak Life Into Your Soul

Choose one affirmation each day, write it at the top of your journal page, and reflect on how it applies to your life. Let your words flow without judgment. This is your space to heal.

Affirmation Prompts:

1. **"I am worthy of love, peace, and protection."**
   - What has kept me from believing this?
   - What evidence can I find that I am, in fact, worthy?

2. **"I forgive so I can be free."**
   - Who am I still holding hostage in my heart?
   - What would it feel like to release that burden?

3. **"My past does not define my value."**
   - What painful moments have shaped how I see myself?
   - How can I begin to rewrite that story?

4. **"I choose to heal, even when it hurts."**
   - What does healing mean for me right now?
   - Where do I need to be brave in my healing journey?

5. **"Every day, I am becoming more of who I truly am."**
   - What parts of me have I hidden or silenced?
   - How can I start showing up fully as myself?

6. **"I am happy, healthy, wealthy, and wise."** *(My personal favorite!)*
   - What area of my life needs the most attention right now?
   - What action step can I take to align with this affirmation?

You are not behind. You are not broken. You are becoming.

Let these reflections and affirmations serve as daily reminders that **your healing is sacred**, and your story—yes, even the painful chapters—can become someone else's hope.

The flame of brilliance burns brightest in the heart of a **comeback champion**. And that champion? She's you.

Final Encouragement: I want to share how to go from painful to purposeful!

Seven Tips to Stay Consistent and Reclaim Your Power

Transitioning from heartbreak to healing isn't a straight line—it's a daily decision. It takes work, faith, and a fierce commitment to yourself. But let me remind you: **You are not what happened to you.** You are what you choose to become next.

Here are seven powerful tips to help you stay consistent, focused, and full of fire as you walk from pain to purpose:

1. Start with a Morning Routine That Centers You

The way you start your day sets the tone for everything. Begin with 10–15 minutes of *you time*—pray, journal, stretch, sip your tea in silence, or speak your affirmations aloud. Start by saying:

"I am grounded. I am focused. I am ready."

Even when your world feels chaotic, your routine can anchor you in peace.

2. Make Small Promises—and Keep Them

Consistency isn't about perfection. It's about building *trust* with yourself. Start small:

- Drink your water.

- Write in your journal.
- Make that one phone call.

Each time you keep a promise to yourself, your confidence grows. Over time, these small wins build a life rooted in integrity and forward momentum.

3. Use Pain as Fuel, Not Chains

Pain will either paralyze you or propel you. The choice is yours. Ask yourself:

"What can I *learn* from this?"
"How can I use this to grow?"

When you shift from *why me* to *what now*, you take your power back.

4. Create a Vision That Pulls You Forward

You can't walk into your purpose without direction. Write out a sharp vision of who you're becoming. What does she look like? What does she do every day? Speak her name and walk like her *today*. Let your future self, lead the way.

5. Protect Your Energy

You can't heal in toxic environments. Set boundaries. Limit your exposure to negative people, heavy conversations, and distractions. Peace is a priority, not a luxury. The more you protect your energy, the more clearly, you'll hear your own voice.

6. Feed Your Mind with Life-Giving Words

Whether it's affirmations, scriptures, or positive audio, surround yourself with messages that breathe life into your soul. Read books that stretch your thinking. Watch content that uplifts, not depletes. Your mind is soil—**plant wisely.**

7. Celebrate Progress, Not Perfection

Healing isn't linear. Some days will be strong. Others will sting. But every step forward—even the shaky ones—counts. Celebrate your courage. Celebrate your decision to keep showing up.

You're not jaded—you're just healing.

You're not trampled—you're being rebuilt.

You're not stuck—you're rising.

Stay consistent. Stay focused. Stay reminded: **the comeback is always greater than the setback.**

You are not just a survivor. You are a **comeback champion.**

E. Celestina Garcia

Executive Coach, M.Ed, ICF PCC certified

https://www.linkedin.com/in/coachcelestina

Celestina has been asking questions since she could speak to understand the world and others around her. This curiosity has led to a life of adventure in learning and travel. She has focused her career on being of service and collaboration with others through human development, leadership, and creating the impossible to be possible. For over twenty years Celestina has guided dynamic leadership opportunities in the nonprofit, educational, and corporate environments. She is passionate about cultivating thriving teams in which intentional planning, authentic collaborations, and creative trailblazing support everyone to live their best life. She spends her time crafting a life adventure with her son on the family's ranch in Northern New Mexico. Celestina has been a life coach for nineteen years and holds a Professional Coaching Certification from the International Coaching Federation. Co-founding a transformational training center in 2010 she supported the organization to reach over 2,000 clients globally. As a transformational trainer she works with individuals, companies, and other thought leaders to evolve outdated societal systems and habits. She currently works for the State of New Mexico as a manager overseeing a statewide team of professional development trainers and educational projects. Celestina is a two time Amazon Best Selling Author for her first anthology book, We Blaze the Trail and her 2023 anthology book, The Choice: That Changes Your Life Narrative.

Because You Can: A Journey Through Grief, Grace, and Growth

By E. Celestina Garcia

The Weight of Hurt

Hurt—true hurt—can be felt in every fiber of your being. It is a unique piece of one's personal journey. It can feel all-consuming and, at times, give the illusion of sitting at the table with death, negotiating terms for a life sentence. The experience of grief and loss is sticky, like tar, and for some, it is downright debilitating.

As with much of life, the path to the other side of deep, suffocating pain is a journey—where your ego, life plans, and body are swept up into the cyclone of an F5 tornado, slammed into the wall of a hurricane, and your shattered remains left stranded on a deserted island. And yet, you somehow gather the remaining specks of resilience and will yourself to pass through the flaming eye of a needle, **emerging as a rare and radiant diamond: the new you**.

By now, you may be reading this and nodding your head "yes," though unsure about the shiny diamond part. I know the feeling. That component can feel fleeting—possibly even impossible. It *is* work to create the emergence of a diamond from the rubble of coal left in the wake of life's disasters. But it's possible nonetheless.

If you are here with a tender heart and a box of tissues, waiting in the room of hope for your number to be called—for a golden nugget of reprieve from trauma, or perhaps wishing for a magic erase tool—I pray that one of the stories in this book brings the connection you seek. And if you're here simply to see what this is all about—wondering what a group of women who have lived through challenging times might contribute—may our words satisfy your curiosity. May they show you how the human experience unfolds and just how resilient the soul can be. May they equip you with tools for any potential storm you may one day face.

And if you are here, ablaze in your spectacular "been there, done that" glory, ready to make that final push through the ring of fire into the lush lilac fields of healed peace, may the linchpin of grace and ease grab hold of every cell in your body and carry you safely to the other side.

Regardless of where you are right now in your journey with life-ing, I'm grateful you are here. I'm so pleased that in this moment, we are connected and blessed to witness the absolute miracle of each other's strength and tenacity—to take one more step forward. To keep choosing into the journey, *because we can.*

This—literally—is the formula for human progress: one more step. Learning to stand. Moving into an unoccupied space with a step. Then choosing, logically and bravely, to take another. When we fall, there's an added component: to dig deep and empower our whole self to rise and engage again. It seems simple. At times, it feels easy. Then, inevitably, we take a risk—or zig when we should have zagged—and the journey gets complicated.

That's when sentiments arise: *ouch, oops, yeah, could've avoided that one, yikes, oh no, darn it, I don't like this, ahhhhh, WTH, why me.* And on rare occasions, the optimist within us might arise to revel in joy at the sight of our symbolic scraped knee and the bulging bump on our forehead from diving headfirst into our life path.

Scars and Scrapes: The Early Lessons

I was that kid who loved to ride my bike with all the neighborhood kids. When we fell off and got scraped up, it was a badge of honor. We'd lift our pant leg or roll up a sleeve, proudly displaying the bloodied knee or elbow like it was treasure. We'd recount how the crash happened—every twist of the handlebars and dramatic tumble shared with pride—how we got up, and how, obviously, we were better riders because of it. We weren't embarrassed. We were strong. We weren't broken—we were brave. **We were *badass*.**

So when did that change? When did we stop celebrating our scars? Maybe it didn't really change. Maybe I just forgot. Maybe we all do, sometimes. Because the war wounds of adulthood—the heartbreaks, betrayals, failures, and breakdowns—are just grown-up versions of those scraped knees. They're still badges of honor. Marks that we lived, that we tried, that we dared to ride fast and fall hard.

And maybe, just maybe, they're meant to be shared too. With our friends, our kids, the ones who look up to us—or even with the reflection in the mirror that needs reminding. Strength doesn't come from staying clean and unscathed. It comes from standing back up—bruised, wiser, still willing to ride. *No matter how messy it gets, we remain the constant in every step we take. The lighthouse guiding our soul back to acceptance. Back to ourselves.*

For eighteen years, I've been called to lead an annual Novena to the Santo Niño de Atocha (nine days of prayer to the Child Jesus). This is my family's patron saint. My ancestors are of Spanish descent and have lived in the United States for approximately fourteen generations. My grandmother's great-great-grandparents, along with family members and the small ranching community of Dahlia, New Mexico, built a small chapel in honor of the Santo Niño. My whole life, I've traveled from wherever I lived to that chapel to pray the rosary and, as my grandmother would say, "visit" the Santo Niño.

As a child, I didn't have a choice in the matter. These hours-long car rides into the red clay countryside were mandatory. In our family, when Grandma said something, you did it—without question. And if you protested, you did so in silence.

Over the years, I came to love those car rides. They were filled with New Mexican music playing in the background, nonstop conversations in Spanglish, and homemade burritos for snacks. Each trip was a day of family, faith, and connection. Until one day, there was one less person in the car.

Our rock. Our best friend. My mentor. The strongest person I knew—gone.

When my grandmother transitioned from this earth, I was no longer a child but a grown adult. That day marked more than just her passing—it marked the moment I had to accept that it was time to grow into the woman she had always seen in me. It was time to find my own path forward, to begin integrating the lessons she had quietly and consistently taught me. She had carved the way through her faith, through her discipline, through the sacred act of teaching me to lead prayer—even if it would take time for me to fully understand the significance. And while I didn't feel ready, didn't feel worthy—while I secretly hoped someone else might step up instead—I knew, deep down, it would be me. Of course it would be me. Because she taught me. She trained me to recognize the call. To feel the pull of responsibility even through doubt. And to show up—not because I was sure, but because I could.

Getting Called and Assigned

Praying the nine-day Novena was never something I set out to do with others. When a friend kindly invited me to join his brother's annual pilgrimage—walking one hundred miles as part of a Catholic Church program—I politely declined. I thought, *there's no way*. Were they serious? I had run a marathon before and knew the pain of 26.2 miles—walking a hundred sounded outrageous. I shrugged it off with a bold, "No thank you. Me and God are good," and moved on. To be honest, by that time at the age of twenty-seven, I was already calling myself a "Cultural Catholic"—a term I coined to describe my ancestral roots and upbringing in Catholicism, even though I no longer aligned with many mainstream, dogmatic Christian teachings. I hadn't left my faith, but I was definitely on a time-out.

Guess what I learned? God doesn't care. God will remind you who's in charge. And the universal power—no doubt in cahoots with my ancestors—put me on the track to bring my ego-driven, "I know better" self back to work.

Just a few weeks later, everything changed. My mother—my lifeline, my anchor, the reason I exist—came home from the doctor with a diagnosis: a brain tumor. At that moment, the idea I had so casually dismissed came rushing back, not as an invitation from a friend, but as a clear and undeniable call from God. Suddenly, walking those one hundred miles from our little family *capilla* to the Santuario de Chimayó wasn't about tradition or obligation—it was about hope. About surrender. About faith. So I leaned into the sacred structure my grandmother had taught me—the nine-day Novena—and began the journey on foot, step by step, praying for a miracle to heal my mother.

Her diagnosis, the unraveling of my extended family as we struggled to stay connected, and the aching absence of my grandmother—our spiritual compass—were the visible reasons I began the pilgrimage. But underneath all that were deeper currents pulling me forward. The silent, unspoken grief I carried. The pain of witnessing trauma in the vibrant layers of my family, my community, my friends. The consequences of my own choices. These were the parts no one saw—the massive underbelly of the iceberg. And it was that hidden weight that finally brought me to lay down my pride and say, ***Okay God—tell me what you want me to do, and show me how to do it.***

I had no more fight left. What I had were the raw and real wounds of everything. And I got the picture. It was time for me to show up—because I could.

I was 27 when I took that first step on the pilgrimage. What I didn't know then was that it would become an annual journey—one that would carry me deeper into healing each year. By my eighth or ninth walk, the road had become more than a physical path—it was a spiritual training ground. Each mile, each novena, was shaping something in me I couldn't fully see yet. Like pressure on coal, year after year, the pain, the prayers, the breaking and rebuilding were slowly making a diamond.

And here's something important: I never got to do these prayer journeys alone. Every year, different people were called in—some from down the street, others from different parts of the world—to walk pieces of the path with me. Sometimes they came with their own prayers, sometimes they came not knowing why they were joining. But they always came. And somehow, I was always the one asked to guide the way—often reluctantly, often wondering *why me*, especially while still doing the inner work myself. But the role of leading others, even through my own healing, became its own kind of sacred assignment.

The exposure to trauma—my own and that of others—was not a one-time event. It has been continuous, layered, sometimes loud and sometimes invisible. Every year I walked, life kept handing me more to carry. And still, I kept walking.

The Iceberg We Carry

Let me put it this way: as a coach and trainer helping others manifest their dreams, I was once asked to lead a workshop on grief and loss. My opening slide listed just a fraction of the lived experiences— mine, my family's, my community's—that shaped me. With a network of 45 aunts and uncles and nearly 500 cousins, the stories run deep and wide. Here's a taste of that list (in no particular order): childbirth complications, poverty, drought, animal deaths, cancer, addiction, suicide, police brutality and murder, domestic violence, false imprisonment, racial discrimination, school shaming, professional glass ceilings, drunk driving victims, ignored educational needs, rape, natural disasters (fires, floods, tornadoes), car theft, murder, gag orders, predatory lending, illiteracy, PTSD, exposure to

Agent Orange, military service, death of loved ones, brain tumors, car accidents, divorce, business failures, depression, anxiety, apathy—and yes, even being alienated by loved ones who couldn't or wouldn't make room for my growth, who saw my success as a threat instead of a shared win.

That list? That's the underbelly of the iceberg. That's the grit that shaped the diamond. So when I speak of hurt, please know I've lived it. I've witnessed it. I've prayed through it. And I've coached and trained people across the world on how to walk through it too—to acknowledge, release, and transform it.

Because healing doesn't mean we never break—it means we learn to take another step. We learn to stand back up. *And we remember: we all can. You can, I promise, it's true.*

The lessons I share in the rest of this chapter? They aren't theories. They're what I've learned from every blistered mile, every unexpected companion, every prayer whispered in pain or power. They're the diamonds I've been shaped into—and the tools I now offer with open hands.

Know this: there is no "free pass" in life. No amount of "being good" or "doing it right" will exempt you from carrying your own cross. I've tried all three—and protested plenty. But watching others go through it doesn't grant immunity. **You still have to walk your own path.** The only way to create your purpose—your diamond—is to go through it, step by step.

Tools for the Sacred Path

Whatever your beliefs may be, develop a practice of prayer or intentional connection with your source—something you can do anywhere, anytime. Set your intention for the road ahead to be filled with grace, ease and love. Acknowledge that *you are a miracle right now*, just as you are. Forgive and release anything that has ever held you back. And express gratitude—for every blessing, big or small, and for all the abundance on its way.

Get a journal or tool to reflect and write out:

- Your life purpose (ask God, your angels, your inner voice to guide you).
- Your top five values (get specific).
- The unique value you bring to the world.
- What you are willing to give up or change in order to create the life of your dreams.
- Three to five people who serve as your "bumper guards", your "phone a friend" list on this journey—those who know, notice, and champion you, whether you're a lump of coal or a polished diamond.

Note: this list may and probably will evolve as you do. Life events will shape your needs, and your circle of support shifts right along with it. Never were the exact same people, in the exact same way, a part of the annual novena. Never were the exact same needs or breakdowns experienced from year to year. This is how the journey of life keeps us on our toes and gifts us new opportunities to meet people where they and we are at. We are constantly evolving and growing so never are your days, your opportunities to take another step through whatever you are moving through, the same. It's why we reload our rations, creature comforts, spaces of pause, and gear for the next leg of this life journey at each pit stop of grace.

In the process through the hurt and pain, acknowledge your pain points. They are not detours—they are the breakdown before the breakthrough. They will be messy, difficult, and meant to test you in all the ways that push growth. Most people don't run toward change; they're pulled into it by the momentum of purpose.

So if you're going through it, congratulations, my friend—you are exactly where you need to be. Take a deep breath. Peel yourself off the bed, the couch, or the floor. Drink some water. Keep breathing. **And take your next step forward...*because you can.***

And when you do, take a moment to look at your scars—not with shame, but with pride. Just like we used to do as kids, lifting our pant legs to show off our battle wounds from a bike crash, these life scars are proof that you showed up, that you tried, that you lived. They're the receipts of your resilience. The markers of your badassness. They are not the opposite of success—they *are* success. Your story, bumps and bruises included, is what makes your path a living, breathing adventure. And the fact that you're still here? Still stepping forward? That's more than enough reason to be proud.

And if you're wondering whether the diamond is real—whether it's possible to emerge from deep pain with something beautiful to show for it—**I'm here to tell you: *yes, it is.*** I am that diamond. Not flawless. Not untouched. But strong, radiant, and whole in a way I never imagined possible when I was sitting in the wreckage.

There were many days I couldn't see the reason for the breakdowns I was walking through. I questioned God. I felt abandoned. I wondered if peace would ever return. But here's what I've learned: while we may not always understand the why—and while the safety of God's protection may sometimes feel distant—the journey always reveals what we need. The right glimmers of hope. The right people. The unexpected wisdom. The strength for just one more step.

And then one day, often without warning, you realize the pain no longer lives in the same place. You've moved through the eye of the needle. You've reached the other side—maybe not all at once, but little by little. Forgiveness doesn't always arrive in a sweeping moment. Sometimes it takes years. And that's okay. That's why we pack a spiritual toolbox. That's why we reset as many times as needed. Because healing has no deadline—and becoming the diamond is a process worth every single step.

The Miracle, and the Message

And yes—my mother is alive and well today. Tumor-free. Fully healed. That miracle? It came. Not just through prayer or the miles walked, but through the collective faith, hope, and love poured in by every single person who showed up along the way.

Each year, countless miracles unfold on that sacred path—some witnessed in undeniable ways, others quietly confirmed in the heart of the one who prayed.

Eighteen years have passed—many marked by the full hundred-mile journey, others shaped uniquely to meet the moment, the season, and the needs of those called to participate.

And with every step, the truth deepens: those who walk beside us— some literally, some spiritually, some simply through a word or a whisper of prayer—become part of the miracle too.

We become together.

So here's to the sacred path we each walk, and the times our paths intersect to shine light for one another—reminding us that we only ever need to show up, one step at a time. Because we can.

To every teacher on this winding road—thank you.

To the moments that cracked me open—thank you.

To the divine orchestration that allowed me to rise from the rubble with clarity, compassion, and calling—thank you.

I'm here because of this collective work we are all called to do.
To bring our spirit forth.
To embody this fleeting window of time and call it love.
To walk through the shadows and the storms and still choose to blaze.
To remember who we are—*A fire. A light. A diamond forged under divine pressure.*

We are meant to experience all life brings. We are meant to heal. We are meant to lead.

So if you're reading this wondering if it's your time: *it is.*

If you're wondering if you're ready: *you are.*

And if you're wondering if you're alone: *you're not. I'm right here.*

Because we can, we take the next step.
We forge the diamonds within our souls.
We fuel the flame. We write our names in the stars.

Ultimately, we are meant to rise and step forward...because we can. And so it is.

Lee Ruocco

Sweet Addiction LLC
Owner/Operator

https://www.facebook.com/lee.ruocco.3
https://www.instagram.com/lee.ruocco.39/

I'm a proud mom of two, a Pastry Chef, and a recovering addict living in North Carolina. For years, I struggled with addiction and the chaos that came with it, but recovery gave me the chance to rebuild my life—and become the mother, business owner, and woman I always wanted to be. I now run a custom cake business where I get to pour creativity and love into every dessert I make. But more than anything, I'm passionate about sharing my story in hopes that it reaches someone who needs it. Whether you're in your own battle or watching someone you love struggle, I want you to know you're not alone. Recovery is hard, but it's possible —and worth every step. If my story can help just one person feel less alone, then everything I went through has meaning.

Forgiving the One Who Hurt Me Most

By Lee Ruocco

Eight months after my son was born, I checked myself back into treatment.

I had white-knuckled my way through my entire pregnancy—no drugs, no alcohol, just grit, willpower, and the desperate hope that I could rewrite the story of my life. Every day had felt like a war between the person I was trying to become and the person I used to be. I went to prenatal checkups, kept my head down, ate when I could, and tried not to drown in the echo of my past. But postpartum depression doesn't care about how strong you think you are. It doesn't care how many promises you make or how many months you've stayed clean. It doesn't care that you've become a mother or that you're hanging on by a thread. It seeps into your bones quietly, slowly, until one morning you wake up and you don't recognize your own thoughts. You feel yourself slipping, but you don't know how to stop it. Or if you even can.

I wasn't sleeping. I wasn't eating. I couldn't keep up with the noise in my head, nor could I silence it. There were days I sat in the nursery, staring blankly at the wall, trying to will myself into feeling something other than fear and failure. The love I had for my son was real—overwhelming and pure—but it was tangled in a fog I couldn't fight through. I was terrified. Not just of postpartum depression, but of myself. The old version of me. The addict. The girl who self-destructed at the first sign of pain. The one who ran when things got too real. I could feel her getting louder, closer to the surface as she clawed her way back. I was terrified she was going to rip everything away from me—again.

So, I did something that felt like defeat. Felt like failure. I asked for help.

Again.

It wasn't my first time in treatment. I was a seasoned regular in the rehab world—familiar with the routines, the nonstop support groups with their usually uncomfortable chairs and whiteboards filled with therapeutic acronyms. The motivational posters of clichés that once felt cheesy, but now rang true in every avenue of my story. I had been in and out of facilities for years. I knew how to talk the talk, to nod in all the right places, to throw out phrases like "cognitive distortions" and "self-sabotage" like I believed them. I had learned how to survive treatment. What I hadn't learned—what I had avoided every time—was how to actually do the work.

I'd never been to this facility before. We had moved to the area right before our son was born, but I could tell right off the rip which counselors were soft and which ones would call you on your bullshit. I thought I would be able to manipulate my way through this place just like I had every other time I'd been in treatment. But what I didn't know was that this place was going to change and reshape everything I knew about myself. I thought I knew who I was. I thought I knew my limits and what I could handle. But nothing had prepared me for what it would really mean to start working the 12 Steps for the first time—not just reciting them, not just pretending, but actually digging in. Getting a sponsor and being completely open and honest with someone, no bullshit. No more pretending. No more faking it. Pretending never kept me clean, and faking it never fixed the broken pieces inside of me. I needed to actually do the work—the real, gut-wrenching, soul-cracking work.

At first, I assumed Step Nine—making amends—would be the hardest. I imagined all the people I had hurt, all the bridges I had burned, and all the trust I had shattered. I braced myself for uncomfortable phone calls, awkward letters, heavy silences on the other end of the line, and, of course, rejection. I pictured trying to explain why I did what I did, when even I didn't fully understand it.

But what I didn't realize, what I couldn't have known, was that those conversations—while humiliating and painful—would be nothing compared to the one I'd have to have with myself.

Forgiving other people is hard.

But forgiving yourself?

That's a whole different war. One I'd never fought.

It's one thing to say sorry to the people you've wronged. It's another to look in the mirror and say, "I forgive you," and not flinch. To mean it. To say it without qualifiers or conditions or the desperate hope that someone else will validate it. To say it, not because you want to feel better, but because you want to be better.

I had spent most of my life apologizing. For the chaos I caused, for the lies I told, for the promises I broke. "I'm sorry" was my reflex, my armor, my mask. I said it so often it lost its meaning—even to me. I used apologies like band-aids, slapping them on wounds I had no intention of healing. But this time, in treatment, it was different. I wasn't just asked to say I was sorry. I was asked to find out why I did the things I did. I was asked to stop hiding behind the stories I told myself and start telling the truth.

Step Four was where the unraveling began.

A searching and fearless moral inventory of ourselves.

Those words still haunt me. Not because of what they asked me to do, but because of what they forced me to see. I sat with a notebook in my lap and started writing. At first, it felt mechanical. Lists of things I had done. Names. Events. But somewhere in the middle of that mess, I hit a nerve. And everything began to bleed.

I wasn't just making a list—I was pulling up the floorboards of my soul. I wrote until my hand ached and my eyes burned. I wrote down every lie, every betrayal, every time I chose drugs or destruction over love or stability. I wrote about the men I used to feel powerful around. The people I manipulated because I didn't know how to be vulnerable. I wrote about the nights I told myself I was fine while silently begging someone to notice I wasn't. I wrote about the shame I carried like a second skin, and how I believed—deep down—that I was unlovable. Broken. Unfixable.

And that's when I realized: I didn't need to be forgiven by others nearly as much as I needed to forgive myself.

I had been my own worst enemy for years. I had sabotaged anything and everything good. I had run from healing because I believed I didn't deserve it. I had punished myself for things long after everyone else had moved on. I wore guilt like a trophy, convinced that if I just held onto it long enough, it would mean I was sorry enough.

But guilt isn't the same as growth. And shame is not a strategy.

I remember one of the counselors saying, "You can't heal in a place you're still trying to escape." That hit me hard. I had spent so much time running—from pain, from truth, from responsibility. But mostly, from myself. "Change your people, places, and things." Something we hear a lot in recovery. But none of that really mattered. Every city I moved to, every relationship I jumped into, every relapse—I told myself I was starting over, but I never really left the wreckage behind. I carried it with me. Because the real problem wasn't out there.

It was in me.

The person I needed to face wasn't my ex, or my parents, or my old friends.

It was the girl in the mirror.

She terrified me. Because I knew what she was capable of. I knew how far she could fall. But I also knew she was still in there— somewhere. Bruised and battered, yes. But not beyond saving.

There was one night during treatment, long after lights-out, when I sat alone in the corner of the group room. It was quiet—eerily so. Most of the girls had gone to bed, but I couldn't sleep. My mind was racing. I stared at the wall, the laminated slogans—"One day at a time," "Let go and let God"—all blending together. I felt hollow. Like a ghost in my own life.

I picked up a dry-erase marker and walked over to the board. Without really thinking, I wrote:

"You are the problem. But I forgive you."

I stared at it for a long time. The dry-erase marker was trembling slightly in my hand. Those words, they looked hollow at first, like they didn't belong to me—like they were meant for someone braver, someone more whole. My chest ached as I stared at them, trying to believe they could be true. They felt like both a wound and a balm. It was the first time I had ever said that to myself. Out loud. On purpose.

And in that moment, something shifted.

Then, I reached into my Big Book and pulled out the worn photograph I always kept tucked inside its pages. It was my son, his face so pure, so wide-eyed and untouched by the weight of the world. He looked like hope. Like everything good I ever wanted but never thought I deserved. I traced the edges of the picture with my fingers, as if I could feel his little hand in mine. That tiny smile—so unaware of the chaos I had come from—reminded me why I was really here.

I wanted more than just sobriety. I wanted a future. *His* future. I wanted to be there to teach him how to tie his shoes and ride a bike, how to be kind in a cruel world, how to love himself without shame. I wanted to be present for every moment: scraped knees, late-night talks, heartbreaks, triumphs. I wanted to be the kind of mother who didn't miss a thing—not because I was perfect, but because I stayed. Because I fought.

But forgiveness? Forgiveness wasn't a moment. It wasn't something I could write down and will into existence. It wasn't a switch I could flip. It was a long, slow burn. A quiet, aching process that peeled back the layers of guilt I had wrapped around myself like armor. It hurt. God, it hurt. But as I looked at that picture, I knew—I had to walk through that pain if I ever wanted to be the mother he needed. The mother he deserved. That night, something inside me shifted. It was subtle, like the first crack of light at dawn, but I felt it. A softness where there had only been despair. For the first time in what felt like forever, I felt something close to hope—fragile, flickering, but real. And in that quiet moment, I let myself believe, even if only for a breath, that maybe I wasn't destined to keep reliving the same pain. Maybe I could break the cycle. Maybe I could become someone new.

That maybe healing was possible.

That maybe I was worthy of it.

The rest of the steps weren't easy either. Nothing about recovery ever is. But once I stopped trying to outrun my shame and started holding space for it, I found clarity. And in that clarity, I found strength. Real strength—not the kind you fake with smiles and "I'm fine", but the kind you build from the inside out. Quiet. Steady. Honest.

Almost six years later, my life looks completely different. Not perfect. Not easy. But honest. Whole. Real.

I have my son in my life again—and now, a daughter, too. My partner and I are back together, not because we forgot the past, but because we faced it. We rebuilt from the rubble. I own my business. I'm working toward getting my license back. I'm trusted now—by others, and more importantly, by myself.

I can look in the mirror now and not wince.

I see a woman who fought like hell to become someone new. Someone whole. Someone worthy.

Not because I never messed up, but because I finally forgave myself for all the ways I did.

Forgiveness was never about excusing my mistakes. It was about learning from them. About breaking the cycle. About setting myself free.

Because without self-forgiveness, recovery becomes a life sentence of guilt.

But with it?

With it, recovery becomes a new beginning.

A way back to myself.

A way forward into a life worth living.

And that is what I hold onto every day:

Forgiveness is how we begin again.

Forgiveness is how we go beyond the hurt.

Linda Downey

Founder and CEO of Linda Downey Coaching

https://www.linkedin.com/in/linda-downey-625b95140/
https://www.facebook.com/lindadowneycoaching/
https://www.instagram.com/lindadowneycoaching/
https://www.lindadowneycoaching.com/

Linda has worked in the health and wellness field for 40 years. Her training as a Functional Diagnostic Nutrition Practitioner, Whole Life Coach and Heartmath Practitioner combines tools from the fields of Neuroscience, Transformational Psychology, Mindfulness and Nervous System Activation. Using trauma-informed somatic practices and energy modalities also enhances her unique approach to empowering women to live a life they love - free of overwhelming stress and a painful past. From her own life experiences of growing up in an alcoholic household, losing her mother at the age of four, multiple health challenges including autoimmune conditions, the loss of her daughter after 15 years of catastrophic medical issues and the ending of her marriage - it is true life experience and compassion that Linda brings with her education into to her work with clients.

The Gift of Loss

By Linda Downey

The whole week leading up to my daughter's memorial service was surreal, even after 15 years of thinking about the possibility of this day. When you have a child born medically fragile, who spends most of her life in the hospital, facing one catastrophic diagnosis after another, you think you have prepared yourself. You haven't. But there was something I was even more unprepared for, that hit like a tractor-trailer I didn't see coming. In that moment at her service, there was a shift in the walls I had built, the anger and resentment I held towards the only other person grieving in the same way I was. Charlotte's father.

When I think back to my first awareness of Mike's affair, it was probably around 2006, when my son Corey was 4 and Charlotte was 2. Have you ever lived through an infidelity in a relationship? There is a place where you just... know. There is no real proof yet, nothing tangible like a picture or a text. There is just a feeling that, if paid attention to, is really a knowing. Probably that means the betrayal has been going on for some time, or maybe that varies. I don't know about that. I just know the breakdown of our relationship, and the building of the walls became noticeable enough, like a humming thread of judgment and resentment that ran through the trips to the ER in the middle of the night. The more I felt threatened and alone and fearful, the more I controlled, pushed, and judged. And the more I did that, the more he disappeared, checked out even when home, and buried himself in whatever.

During those years from 2006 or so to 2019, when Charlotte finally passed, I had a really strong case built for how wronged I was, how hard I worked, how alone I felt, how bad I had it. I was the one who did 95% of the hospital runs. I was the one whose day blew up when her O2 tanked, or her retching started. I made all the appointments. I did the regular visits with the kidney doctors, the cardiologist, pulmonary, GI, and eventually oncology. I did the therapy visits for speech and OT and PT. I went for the fittings for the wheelchair and other adaptive equipment.

Mike did some of those, occasionally, when I couldn't for some reason. He arranged his schedule to go directly from work at night to sleep with her when she was inpatient, which meant going from New Jersey to the Children's Hospital of New York every night for what was often months at a time. Charlotte never stayed at the hospital for a quick visit. If she came home in under 10 days, we felt like it barely counted as an admission. Two or three weeks gave the impression of "Not bad, that was a quick one." Mostly, she was there from 1–5 months—some years, that happened a couple of times a year.

When a sense of stability showed up, and Charlotte had much more well/home time, Mike took her places. It might be to a petting zoo, or to see the hot air balloon festival. On good weather days, he hooked her "chariot" up to the back of his bike and they headed off to the park for a bike ride. Sometimes, he sat and put nail polish on her hands on rainy Saturdays. I left the house typically early during the week, around 6:45 a.m., and he would get her ready for school and drop her off on his way to work. He did her hair. Helped her pick her clothes. As a special needs kid, she did not walk or talk (a massive stroke after her open heart surgery at birth caused much damage). But she had strong opinions—about everything! And they had their own games of clothes and hair, what jacket to wear, and songs to sing on the way to school. As a professional photographer, he captured all of those moments in images. Thousands of them. Laughing, singing, sleeping on his chest at the hospital, walking into school. And like many dads, he posted his photos and shared their time together on his IG and FB profiles. People loved the photos. So many had rallied around us when she was born and rushed by ambulance from the hospital in NJ to the critical care neo-natal unit of NY Presbyterian on that pivotal night. Now, they exclaimed how great she looked. They sent love and best wishes. They told Mike what a great dad he was. They rooted for her, for him, for us.

As I watched those comments and looked at the photos, most of which I was not in, my resentment grew. Could I have been in them? Absolutely. Had he asked me to go at times on the different outings—yes, he certainly had, especially in the earlier years. But I chose to have my own "downtime" when he picked up the reins. I took a nap, or grabbed some exercise, or read a book. I told myself I needed the break, and so I took it. After enough time of "needing a break," he stopped asking. He didn't talk much about the adventures when they got home. He didn't call me from the hospital to tell me she finally fell asleep. Maybe he sent a text. But my resentment stopped me from participating even more. I would see his photos online, read the comments, and think, "Sure, he took her to the park, but I took her to the ER." When his extramarital relationship was a certainty, somewhere around 2009, I noticed every absence as a transgression. In my head, I imagined everyone knowing that he was actually having an affair while I was doing all of the hard stuff. That he was having fun while I was suffering. It felt good—even in my own head—to disparage him for all of the hurt, all of the loneliness, all of the anger I carried.

And then, it was over. She passed. We watched every day that week, knowing somehow that this hospital visit would be the final one. We hoped for better news from the doctors each day, but instead got more and more certain this was it. Her 15th birthday was a Thursday that year, and she spent it in the hospital. She was receiving dialysis, and the catheter was being very finicky. It would stop working. It clotted. The alarms went off regularly, and the session would have to be terminated. But on her birthday, she was happy and having fun as the nurses celebrated her. They danced and colored pictures with her. They brought her fun, extra-big birthday glasses, and she laughed and kept them on. It was a great day, except for that damn catheter.

On Friday, the hospital called us—something was wrong, and they were not sure what was going on. O2 dropped. BP was erratic. All vitals started going haywire. By Saturday morning, she was on a vent and in a coma. And there she stayed.

Each day that week, I traveled the hour-plus drive to New York and sat at her bed. Spoke to her doctors. They scratched their heads. She was having multiple mini-seizures per minute, and at this point, Neurology had her on five different seizure meds, none of which made a difference. Seizures had never been one of her issues. Ever. They could not figure it out. As I sat next to my baby, like I had literally dozens of times before with her on a vent and in a coma, I knew it was different this time. I could almost feel her spirit check out. We all held out like that until Sunday, when it was decided that it was time to stop artificially keeping her BP up. Stop reviving a system that was shutting down. Along with her brother, we surrounded her, and I have to believe she knew in some dimension, on some level, that we were there.

What had started in those days following her birthday continued in the days after her death. The resentment and the distance and the walls didn't matter. No one on earth could understand what that week felt like except us. So, my own internal shift of loss, grief, and need had started. And that's when I found myself in the surreal experience of greeting people at my own daughter's memorial service.

There were many impressions from those 2 days. Her wake on Friday night and her Celebration of Life on Saturday. The gathering of over 400 people for a girl who didn't speak and couldn't walk without much support. Three doctors from the Nephrology Department of the hospital made the trip out for her service. Liam, the volunteer guitar player who gave his time two days a week to go from room to room and play for the children, took the train out to NJ from the city to play throughout her service on Saturday. The head of Pediatric Thoracic Surgery waited patiently at the end of the line to give his condolences. He had been instrumental in keeping her alive the day after she was born, and had done multiple procedures and surgeries on her during her 15 years.

Boys and their families from my son's high school. Board members from different organizations that had supported us during her life, especially during the most difficult situations and hospitalizations, cried with us as different people stood up and spoke about how our girl had changed their lives.

But the most impactful impression I had, as I numbly greeted people coming to give their condolences, was made by the images on the video Mike had made that were looping for hours. The video of her life. I saw the happy, smiling girl petting the animals. I saw the look of wonder as she watched the balloons go up. I saw how safe she looked, asleep on her father's chest. I saw the love in her eyes as he hugged her. I saw her pride in her fingernails after he painted them. I saw her concentration when they colored together. I saw her fresh "little girl-ness" as they headed off to school.

As I watched the video over and over during those two days, I saw other parts of her life I had not been paying attention to. I saw the child, not the patient. I saw the little girl, not the survivor. I saw a dad who loved as hard as he could and a man who did the best he could— not the cheater. I saw how my walls and resentment and stress and exhaustion were a contribution to the whole breakdown. I saw how much I had pushed him away as I micro-managed everything. I saw that no single choice comes from a single thought, but rather from a multitude of thoughts, emotions, behaviors, and decisions that are affected and directed by more than one person. I saw Beyond The Hurt.

That evening, we went to get some food with our son and some extended family. The crowds had gone home. The coffin had closed.

There was nothing in the space for me except a yearning to heal. That did not mean go backward. It did not mean start again, new. It meant looking deeply in the mirror. Sit with all that was and all that had been. Use it—don't step over it. Don't mitigate it, and also don't revere it. Just see it for what it was, and from there, step into the possibility and process of forgiveness. The process of crafting a new life. Without Charlotte. Not as life partners, but as co-parents of our son, as two people who had lost a child together. As adults who owned the responsibility fully for the path of our relationship, regardless of the choices of the other. That started with me saying, "I am so sorry I never gave you the credit for all that you did for Charlotte. I saw so clearly today how I gave her the medical access and you gave her a childhood." His response was—"She needed both, and we both gave what we could for all of it."

Seeing the whole picture from a much higher lens was critical for me to see it more clearly. Forgiveness is not about condoning someone else's choices. It's not about saying now everything is okay, let's forget about it all. But it is saying what is the lesson here for me, and how do I set myself free through forgiveness—of myself, of Mike, of the loss, of the pain that life often is. What is there for me to learn from it all, so that the rest of life continues to expand and fulfill me? I am grateful that Mike has stayed a close friend as we lead our separate lives.

Sonia Rodrigues

Transition to Wellness
Psychotherapist & Life Transition Coach

https://www.linkedin.com/in/sonia-rodrigues-48b87149/
https://www.facebook.com/SoniaRodriguesLPC/
https://www.instagram.com/transition.to.wellness/
www.transitiontowellness.com
https://soniarodrigues-marto.tribesites.com/

Sonia Rodrigues-Marto has been a licensed psychotherapist for 20 years. She is the owner of a psychotherapy and coaching practice called Transition to Wellness. She has worked with people of all ages, helping them navigate various challenges in their life. She utilizes a holistic approach and provides a safe and supportive environment where her clients can feel supported on their path towards healing from their traumatic experiences and she guides them towards creating the life they desire. She provides individual therapy and coaching and also offers a variety of presentations on topics related to trauma, post-traumatic growth and fostering resilience.

Your Inner Compass:
Intuition and the Journey to Healing

By Sonia Rodrigues

There are moments in life when the ground beneath your feet vanishes—not just metaphorically, but in a way that leaves your body trembling and your mind doubting what's real. For me, that moment came when I learned of my husband's long-term affair. Years of shared dreams, whispered promises, and family milestones dissolved into a whirlwind of betrayal and secrets. The life I thought I had built was swept away, leaving behind a haunting silence. What's worse, the signs were there—but they weren't etched in text messages or found in hidden receipts. They lived in the quiet misalignment of my soul. For years, I kept searching for some concrete evidence that what I was feeling was on point, but I couldn't find anything. I later found out that I didn't find anything, not because it wasn't happening, but because it was being methodically and consciously deleted each and every day in an effort to keep me from finding out the truth.

At first, I didn't understand it. There were no flashing red lights, no confessions, no irrefutable proof. Just a sinking feeling. A tightening in my chest. A subtle but persistent knowing that something was off. My mind and body—once in sync—began to feel divided. I couldn't explain it. I only knew that peace had been replaced with restlessness, and that despite the mask of normalcy I wore daily, I was struggling inside, not able to identify what it was that was causing me to feel so uneasy.

It took time for me to recognize that what I was feeling wasn't anxiety, paranoia, or self-doubt. It was intuition. It was the quiet, sacred voice within me speaking louder than any tangible evidence ever could. It was my intuition telling me, *Something is wrong here.*

While I couldn't pinpoint it, I was acutely aware of the disconnect I was feeling in my life and from my partner at the time. I just knew something was extremely off.

My intuition had been whispering to me for years—soft, persistent feelings that something was off. I couldn't explain it, and I couldn't prove it, but the sense of unease never fully left. I searched and searched for answers, trying to make sense of what I felt without any visible evidence to support it. I questioned myself constantly, wondering if I was overreacting, too sensitive, or imagining things. And then, after years of quiet inner conflict, I found it—that one undeniable piece of truth that shattered everything. In a single moment, I saw clearly what I had felt all along: the very person I thought I could trust, the person I had built a life and home and family with, had been betraying that trust in a way so deep and painful that it was almost unspeakable. I couldn't even look at him the same. When I did, it felt like I was staring into the face of a stranger. The man I thought I knew was gone—or maybe, he was never who I believed he was. In the aftermath, I questioned everything: my memories, my choices, even my reality. But amidst that unraveling, I also began to do something I hadn't done before—I leaned into my intuition. I stopped dismissing it. I began to listen with reverence. And slowly, that quiet voice—the one I had ignored for so long—became the guide that led me back to myself. It became the starting point of my healing.

When the Truth Shatters You

The truth eventually surfaced—cruelly, explosively, and with finality. He had been living a double life for years. The man I had loved, trusted, and built a future with had betrayed me in the most intimate way. I wish I could tell you I felt relief when I finally knew the truth, but that would be a lie. What I felt was devastation. Rage. Shame. I blamed myself for not seeing it sooner, for staying too long, for ignoring the whispers of my soul.

But here's what I know now: trauma blinds us. It stifles our inner voice with fear, with a desperate clinging to hope, with the need for something—anything—to still feel real.

Divorce is not just a legal process. It is a death—a thousand little deaths. It's the end of shared morning coffees, of texts that once made you smile, of anniversaries, and family traditions. But what made my divorce particularly painful was not just the separation, but the betrayal—the deception that rewrote every memory we had made. I grieved not only the loss of my marriage but also the loss of my reality.

The Awakening of Intuition

What I want women to understand—and what I wish someone had told me—is that intuition is not something mystical or far-fetched. It's not a special gift reserved for a few. It is an ancient, internal compass that lives in each of us—a quiet, wise voice that becomes clearer and more trustworthy the more we learn to honor it, listen to it, and respond with care.

For years, I doubted myself. I brushed aside the quiet warnings and soft urgings inside me because they didn't come with proof. I told myself I needed evidence, facts, logic. I let reason silence what my body was gently trying to say. And in doing so, I betrayed myself again and again. That was my first wound—not trusting the part of me that always wanted to protect and guide me.

Healing began when I stopped looking for clarity and reassurance outside of myself and started turning inward with curiosity and tenderness. I began to realize that the voice inside me—the one I had ignored for so long—was still there, still speaking, still waiting patiently to be heard.

One morning, months after the separation, I stood in front of the mirror. I barely recognized the woman staring back at me. Her eyes looked tired—tired from carrying too much for too long. Her smile felt like a performance. But in that moment of honesty and stillness, I whispered to her: "You knew it. The whispers were right." That single sentence cracked something open in me. It wasn't just a realization—it was a remembering. A moment of deep self-recognition. And I made a vow that day: *never again*. Never again would I let someone convince me to doubt what I feel. Never again would I ignore the quiet wisdom that lives within me.

And for those of you who may not know what gaslighting is—please learn about it. It's a form of emotional manipulation that can leave you second-guessing your instincts, your feelings, and your memories. Understanding it gave me the language to reclaim my truth. Learn to recognize the signs early. You deserve to feel safe and certain within yourself.

From that day forward, I began to measure people not only by their words, but by how I felt in their presence. Did I feel calm? Seen? Respected? Or did something in me tense up, shut down, or feel small? I started listening to the energy behind the words. I noticed how my breath changed, how my body reacted, how peace either settled in or disappeared. I paid attention to the subtle cues—because they were never really subtle. I had just been taught not to notice them.

And here's what I want you to know: *energy does not lie.* When something feels off, it usually is. That unsettled feeling, that hesitation, that quiet nudge—it's your inner guidance trying to protect you. Intuition is a powerful, steady presence within you. It is your inner compass, your quiet guide, and your fiercest protector. It doesn't need to be proven to be real, and it doesn't ask for permission to exist. You don't have to explain it to anyone. You simply have to honor it and let it guide you. It has always been there, patiently waiting for you to remember its strength.

Rebuilding from the Rubble

In the beginning, the journey of healing felt impossible. I was exhausted—emotionally, spiritually, physically, and when I wasn't exhausted, I was in utter shock at the rubble that was my life. I could not stop thinking about how I would ever trust someone again. But little by little, I began to recreate a very new and different chapter in my life. Not the life I had before or the life I had originally imagined, but one that felt empowering and freeing. I was no longer stuck in a situation where I felt like something was terribly wrong, but I could not pinpoint what it was, nor could I stop it.

Movement became my medicine. I found dance—initially just as a way to connect with others and to have something fun to do, but it turned into something far more powerful. Dance gave me a way to reclaim my life and reconnect with something I was really passionate about, to express myself, and to find true joy in moving my body. It was a place where I could focus on moving to the beat and not worrying about any of the outside pressures. With each beat, each step, I shed the layers of pain, shame, and disconnection. I wasn't just dancing—I was reconnecting with a part of myself that had gotten lost many years ago. I would often say to myself, *Why would I ever give up doing something that brought me so much joy and peace?* And all I could think was that life got busy, and I rarely ever had time for myself as a working mom who was also in graduate school. I was quickly reminded of the power of connecting with your passions and how healing that could be.

The dance studio became my sanctuary. It was there, among rhythm and laughter, that I met so many people who were also learning to love themselves again. People who had faced heartbreak, loss, and life's unrelenting storms were finally doing something for themselves. It very quickly felt like a family. When I would walk in, everyone would stop what they were doing to greet me, and the owners would come over to give hugs and a warm welcome. Together, we moved, we rooted for one another, and we created a community of support and encouragement. There is true power in connection; it can be the best medicine for a broken heart.

The Sacredness of Support

The most transformative part of my healing came when I began supporting other women walking through similar pain. I didn't plan to focus my therapy practice on women healing from trauma, divorce, domestic violence or betrayal, as they started opening up to me in our sessions, I started to feel more comfortable saying things like, "Trust me, I can genuinely understand what you are going through" or "I know how painful this is for you and your family." And what I discovered was this: when we speak our truth, we give others permission to do the same and a lightbulb goes off and says, "Oh my, I am not alone, you get it, I don't have to be so embarrassed anymore or I don't have to keep this to myself anymore, there are more women out there who have experienced this and understand what I am feeling right now." That was so powerful for me and my clients.

One by one, women began reaching out to me. Some were still in relationships that no longer served them. Others had recently endured betrayal. Many felt lost, broken, and unsure of where to begin. I didn't have all the answers. But I had walked through the fire and survived and was on the path towards renewal.

Eventually, this calling grew into something bigger. I created Transition to Wellness, a space for women navigating the painful yet sacred process of reclaiming their lives and finding their power again as they began to write a new chapter in their own stories.

Lessons from the Ashes

Looking back now, I can see how every fragment of my pain held purpose. That doesn't mean I'm grateful for the betrayal—but I'm deeply grateful for what it taught me.

I learned to trust myself again.

I learned that intuition is not a luxury—it's a lifeline.

I learned that healing doesn't happen alone.

I learned that joy can live alongside grief.

And I learned that love—real, soul-deep love—begins within.

To the woman reading this who is still in the eye of the storm: I see you. I know the ache that grips your chest when the silence becomes unbearable. I know how hard it is to breathe when your world collapses. But I also know this: You are not broken. You are becoming.

Give yourself permission to feel it all. Don't rush the healing. And please, don't wait for the world to validate your intuition. Trust what your body and heart already know.

Finding Joy Again

Today, my life looks nothing like it did back then. And for that, I am profoundly thankful. I wake up to a home filled with light—my sanctuary, designed with intention and love. I dance regularly and let my body move to the music, and the stress melts away. I am surrounded by a tribe of women who uplift me, challenge me, and encourage me. I am supporting other women in their own journeys and helping them navigate their own difficult life transitions, and it feels extremely rewarding.

I've learned to say "no" without guilt, "yes" with joy, and "maybe" when I need space. I've stopped trying to earn love and started choosing it—with discernment, with care, and most importantly, with self-respect.

And yes, I found love again—not just romantic love, but deep, soulful connections rooted in truth and mutual respect. Love that doesn't require shrinking or pretending. Love that feels like home.

You Deserve This, Too

If you take nothing else from my story, let it be this: Your intuition is sacred. When something feels off, honor it. When your soul feels heavy, listen. You don't need the world's approval to walk away from what hurts you. You need only your own permission to choose yourself.

Healing is not linear. Some days will still be hard. But every day is a step closer to the woman you are becoming.

You are not alone.
You are not too much.
You are not to blame.

You are worthy of peace.
You are worthy of joy.
You are worthy of love that honors every part of you.

In Closing

As I sit here, years removed from the chaos that once defined my life, I am filled with awe at how far I've come. And if you are reading this, I believe the same healing is possible for you.

May your intuition always be louder than your fear.
May your body be your guide, your dance, your compass.
May you find your tribe, your truth, and your transformation.

Beyond the hurt, there is hope.
Beyond the betrayal, there is beauty.
Beyond the silence, there is song.

Keep going, beautiful soul.

You will rise above it all and live your best life!

Writing can be a profoundly healing process—an intimate space where thoughts, emotions, and memories can be safely explored and given voice. Through my own healing journey, writing became a lifeline, offering clarity, release, and a path toward self-compassion. As a therapist, I have witnessed the transformative power of written self-reflection in the lives of many women; how putting pen to paper can unlock buried truths, soothe inner wounds, and empower the heart to speak its truth. It is with that deep knowing that I offer these writing prompts—not as a prescription, but as an invitation—to gently explore your inner landscape and support your own unique path to healing.

Writing Prompts

Reconnecting with Intuition

What is intuition to you?

In your own words, define what intuition feels or sounds like. There is no right or wrong answer—only your truth.

Prompt:

"When I think of intuition, I imagine..."
"A time I didn't trust my intuition and what happened was..."
"A time I *did* trust my intuition and it led me to..."

Body Check-In Practice:

Take a quiet moment. Close your eyes. Place one hand on your heart and one on your belly. Breathe deeply.

Ask yourself:

"Is there something in my life right now that feels misaligned?"
"What does my body say when I think about it?"
"If I could silence doubt, what would my inner voice say?"

◎ *Journal the thoughts, emotions, or sensations that arise.*

Honoring the Heartbreak

Betrayal is a rupture, not just of a relationship, but of identity. These prompts can help you process grief with compassion.

Prompt:

"What I lost when my relationship ended was..."
"The hardest part of the betrayal was..."
"What I now understand that I didn't back then is..."

Rebuilding Trust with Yourself

After betrayal, we often stop trusting others, but even more painfully, we stop trusting *ourselves*. This section helps repair that bond.

Self-Trust Reminders:

Listen to my gut feeling
Set and keep boundaries
Say "no" when I need to
Leave when something feels wrong
Choose relationships that support my growth

Prompt:

"The biggest thing that holds me back from trusting myself is..."
"To rebuild that trust, I will start with..."

Moving the Pain Through You

Movement is medicine. It heals what words cannot.

Integrate a Movement Practice:

- A dance playlist that makes you feel powerful and free
- A five-minute stretch in the morning where you listen to your body
- A walk in nature while repeating affirmations aloud

- Joining a class (dance, yoga, martial arts) that allows full self-expression

After your movement practice, use these writing prompts:

"Today, my body taught me…"
"While dancing/moving, I let go of…"
"I now invite in…"

Finding and Nurturing Your Tribe

Healing doesn't happen in isolation. You are not meant to do this alone.

Prompt:

"What kind of support do I *really* need right now?"
"Who in my life makes me feel safe, seen, and supported?"
"Where can I begin to look for aligned connection (women's networks, support groups, dance communities)?"

Connection Challenge:

- Reach out to **one woman** in your life who inspires you, even if it's just a kind message.
- Research one local or online women's group and commit to joining an event or meeting.
- Start a "Support Circle" of 2–3 women going through similar experiences. Create space to share weekly.

Designing a Life Filled with Joy

How can you design a life that welcomes joy in big and small ways?

Prompt:

"What makes me come alive?"
"What did I used to love doing before the relationship that I've forgotten?"

"I will commit to bringing more joy into my week by…"

 A New Chapter

My Healing Declaration:

"I am no longer defined by what broke me.
I trust the whisper of my intuition.
I trust that joy is mine to claim.
I am supported, I am seen, I am rising.
I am whole. I am healing. I am home."

Sign your name and date it.

▦ *Optional: Write a "check-in date" three months from now to revisit your journey.*

Feliz Garcia

Founder and CEO of Feliz Love and Light

https://www.facebook.com/profile.php?id=61574839786000
https://www.instagram.com/felizlovelight/
https://felizloveandlight.com/
https://www.tiktok.com/@felizlovelight?_t=ZT-8xcT9esWOR3&_r=1
https://live365.com/station/Light-the-Way-Radio-a96984

Feliz Garcia's a mom to beautiful twin toddlers, wife, daughter, sister, and active community member. As the creator of the Podcast Sharing Your Miraculous Life with Feliz, my mission is to inspire personal transformation and create a heaven on earth. Through heartfelt conversations, powerful stories, and transformative insights, I aim to build a community rooted in love, light, spirituality, joy, purpose, and happiness. On the podcast we explore what it means to live a fulfilled and miraculous life. Whether we're discussing spiritual practices, sharing personal triumphs, or navigating life's challenges, the podcast serves as a sanctuary for those seeking to infuse more love, positivity, and meaning into their lives. Topics range from the power of forgiveness and living in the present moment, to manifestation, personal transformation, and mindfulness. Feliz recently launched

Light the Way Radio on Live365—an uplifting faith-based radio station shining God's light into the world with encouragement and worship. Join us on this journey of growth, healing, and connection as we work together to cultivate a more joyful and peaceful world.

My Journey of Forgiveness

By Feliz Garcia

I grew up in the beautiful community of Chimayo, in Northern New Mexico. I am the third daughter, the baby of the family (not to mention, the favorite). I like to say I am the baby, the oldest, and the only at the same time because my sisters were 15 and 16 years older than I and went off to college when I was about three.

Growing up, my parents made sure that our family placed value in God, education, the family, love for one another, and involvement in the community. We were taught to share God's love with everyone and help those in need. I was fortunate to grow up in the same community as my grandparents. My grandma, Anita, was a Carmelite devoted to prayer, penance, and service. Her faith and love for her family were a testament to her life for God. My grandma's kindness and love still live with me today. My dad often tells me that I remind him of her. My mom also played a significant role in shaping my faith. She taught me to trust in God and to give my worries to Him, reminding me that His plan is always greater than ours.

As a child, I loved going to Mass at Holy Family Parish in Chimayo. I loved Father Mateo's homilies and the Spanish music during the service. It often brought me to tears, in a good way. I am truly grateful to God for blessing me with such a strong, loving family.

"Dear friends, since God so loved us, we also ought to love one another" (1 John 4:11).

When I was a young child, my cousin was killed along with about 7 other people, including a baby. I can remember that event like it was yesterday, when I was seven years old. I know I was just a little girl, but it impacted my life forever. At that point, I began to realize how ugly this world could be. How could someone kill so many people? This event was so tragic, and it affected me for a long time.

In mid-school, my grandma Anita, my role model, suffered a debilitating stroke that took her life. This was not easy for me. I would think and pray for her every day. I really missed her. The next couple of years, our family continued to experience loss from my other grandma, grandpa, uncle, cousins, and many friends. The hurt and loss just broke me.

But as I got older, I began to realize something: the pain, the anger, the confusion I carried... wasn't hurting anyone but me. Holding onto that grief, that bitterness, only kept me locked in the past, stuck in the dark place.

Since I was a young child, I dreamed of finding my Prince Charming, getting married, and having a family. As the years continued to pass by, I couldn't help but wonder: *Why wasn't I experiencing the love I saw around me? Why did it seem to be so easy for everyone else, but so difficult for me?* In my heart, I knew I was worthy of love, yet it never seemed to come. I was in my late twenties, approaching thirty, and had never experienced the kind of love I had always wished for.

Waiting was difficult, but I trusted that in God's time, I would find the love I had always dreamt of. But as the years kept passing, doubt began to set in, and I started to question whether love was even meant for me after all. I now realize that God was preparing me, not denying me. He was waiting to give me something better than I could have imagined.

"Trust in the Lord with all your heart, and lean not on your own understanding; in all your ways submit to Him, and He will make your paths straight" (Proverbs 3:5-6).

Through all the waiting, loneliness, and disappointment, one thing remained certain: I hadn't forgiven anyone or anything. I had this weight that I was carrying.

"'For I know the plans I have for you,' declares the Lord, 'plans to prosper you and not to harm you, plans to give you a hope and a future'" (Jeremiah 29:11).

For most of my life, I was searching for love in all the wrong places. I stood at my friends' weddings, celebrating their love stories, smiling as they walked down the aisle. I had been a bridesmaid more times than I could count. It felt like I was living out a version of *27 Dresses*, the movie where the main character is always the bridesmaid, but never the bride. In my case, it wasn't a movie, but it sure felt like I was stuck in a real-life version. I was happy for my friends, but deep down, an emptiness grew with each wedding I attended.

It was then that I met my Benito and everything changed! It wasn't just that I had found love, it was that I had found a love that healed me. Benito loved me in a way I had never known before. His love was unconditional. From the moment we met, we both knew that we had found *our* person. He loves me for exactly who I am. That's when I first understood that true love is not just a feeling; it's a choice—a commitment to love, forgive, and support each other, no matter what life throws at us.

Benito taught me the true meaning of forgiveness and the importance of not holding onto anything that no longer serves me. We live by a simple rule: We give each other just five minutes to be upset, and after that, we have to let it go. Over time, I realized how harmful it is to hold onto anger, resentment, or sadness, not only for the person you're upset with but for your own well-being. The more we hold on to these emotions without releasing them, the more they build up, often manifesting as physical illness.

"Bear with each other and forgive one another if any of you has a grievance against someone. Forgive as the Lord forgave you" (Colossians 3:13).

It was through Benito's love that I also learned to forgive myself. For years I carried guilt and shame, blaming myself for everything—

especially things beyond my control. I kept trying to manage every aspect of my life, from being single for so long to not having the family I had always dreamed of. I began to forgive others too, even when I couldn't remember exactly why I had been angry in the first place. Benito's patient love helped me let go of that pain and release the anger I had been holding onto.

For the first time, I understood that to fully receive love, I had to let go of my past mistakes and trust in God's plan for me.

Even after finding love, another challenge arose: infertility. After meeting Benito, I was eager to build a life with him, but my dream of starting a family wasn't coming easily. It felt like yet another test of my faith. I couldn't understand why this had to be so difficult for us. *Why God?* I prayed and prayed, but still, there were no answers. It felt as though I had been waiting my whole life for love, and now, I was waiting, yet again, for the next chapter of my life to unfold. Benito and I had been together for 5 years up to this point.

This period of waiting, confusion, and self-doubt led me to the ACTS (Adoration, Community, Theology, Service) through the Catholic Church, which changed my life forever. It was through this community that I continued to learn to truly forgive myself. I had been carrying so much pain in my heart, and through the ACTS retreat, I learned to release it. The experience helped me confront all the hurt I had kept hidden for so long, even those that I didn't realize I was still holding on to. I thought I had let them go, but truly never laid them at God's feet. I needed to lay them down and truly forgive myself, as God already had. Now, I was able to see how those wounds had manifested in my life, affecting not just my relationships but my entire outlook on the world. The ACTS community gave me the space and support to heal, as well as the courage to let go of the burdens I had carried for so long. It was there that I truly began to understand the power of forgiveness, not just toward others, but toward myself. For me, forgiveness is an ongoing journey.

The ACTS community gave me the space and support to heal, as well as the courage to let go of the burdens I had carried for so long. It was there that I truly began to understand the power of forgiveness, not just toward others, but toward myself. For me, forgiveness is an ongoing journey.

In that waiting, I encountered a new form of forgiveness. I had to forgive myself for the frustration and anger I felt about not having the family I longed for. The disappointment that lingered year after year as we tried to have a baby. At times, I questioned God: *Why wouldn't He give me the dream of becoming a mother when that was all I ever wanted?*

Looking back, I realize how many wonderful people helped me when I needed it most. During COVID, I felt stuck, unsure of what the future held. That was when I was introduced to two extraordinary individuals who walked with me as I released old fears, pain, and the things that were holding me back. Through Jesus, we focused on stepping into the future God had planned for me. Their support opened my eyes to new possibilities.

I'm incredibly grateful for the healing journey we went on together. It felt like a blessing, as though God guided me to them. I had to accept that God's timing was different from mine, and that in His wisdom, He was leading me toward something even greater. Our happiness grew beyond measure when Benito and I were blessed with the miracle of becoming parents to twins.

The journey to bring our twin daughters into the world was far from easy, especially during the pandemic, but it was filled with love and support from our families, friends, and community. It wasn't just my strength and Benito's love that brought our daughters into the world, it was the prayers and support of everyone around us. From prayer warriors to caring members of our community, each person played a part in our journey through their support, encouragement, and faithful prayers. Through their care and prayers, we found the strength to keep moving forward. This is something I will never forget. It reminded me that family, friends, and community are not just important; they're essential. We are not meant to walk through tough times alone. We need others to pray with us, cry with us, and help us carry our burdens.

God's plan for me didn't come immediately, but when it did, it was more beautiful than I could have ever imagined. My daughters, Carolina and Gabriella, are living proof of that. They are a testament to the fact that God's timing is perfect, even when we don't understand it. If I had gotten to receive what I wanted when I wanted it, I would have missed out on the incredible blessing of becoming their mommy. They have changed my life in ways I never thought possible.

"Take delight in the Lord, and He will give you the desires of your heart" (Psalm 37:4).

Looking back, I see how every part of my journey—the waiting, the struggles, the doubts—was leading me to a deeper understanding of God's love and mercy. It wasn't about getting everything I wanted when I wanted it. It was about learning to trust in God's timing, to forgive myself, and to receive His love with an open heart.

Forgiveness isn't just about letting go of anger or bitterness toward others, it's also about letting go of our anger toward God and ourselves. It's about surrendering our plans and trusting that God's plan is better. It's about accepting that sometimes the things we think we want aren't the things that are best for us. And when we surrender, when we forgive, when we trust, peace follows.

Through my journey, I've learned that true love forgives. It forgives the past, the mistakes, and the disappointments. And it chooses to love, no matter what. I've learned to forgive myself, and in doing so, I've discovered how to live a life full of peace and joy. I've learned that God's love is always there, always waiting for us, no matter how far we may have strayed from it.

It took years of waiting, learning, and growing, but now, I see beauty in every part of my story. I am deeply grateful for the love I found in Benito, for the daughters we've brought into the world, and for the incredible community that has supported us along the way. We are never truly alone in our journey, and when we trust in God, He will lead us exactly where we need to be.

This is the story of forgiveness, forgiving myself, forgiving God, and receiving the love that has always been there for me. It's a story of finding peace, of learning that sometimes, the greatest blessings come when we let go of our expectations and surrender to God's will. This is the peace that comes from forgiveness, and it's the peace I want to share with others.

Through my journey of self-discovery, I've learned a few key things that I'd love to share. One of the most profound insights is the power of surrendering to God's plan. When we let go and trust in something greater than ourselves, the results are often more beautiful and fulfilling than anything we could have imagined. This can be difficult, but if we continue to pray for the strength we need in the waiting, His peace and grace will come.

"Be still, and know that I am God; I will be exalted among the nations, I will be exalted in the earth" (Psalm 46:10).

I've come to understand the importance of being authentic, of embracing who we truly are, just as God made us. We are each made in His image, with unique qualities and strengths. Staying true to ourselves allows us to shine brightly in this world.

Letting go of our troubles is crucial, and so is the ability to forgive ourselves for past actions. When we do, we open ourselves to healing and grace. Knowing that God is always with us offers comfort and assurance, reminding us that we are never truly alone.

By embracing these truths, trusting in God's plan, being authentic, letting go, and forgiving ourselves. We can live peaceful, joy-filled lives, guided by divine wisdom. I hope these insights offer encouragement and support as we all seek fulfillment and purpose.

Throughout my journey, I've discovered the vital role of prayer, community, and service in grounding me in God's love. Prayer is incredibly powerful; it's a constant connection to God, offering guidance and comfort. Being part of a community and serving others not only fulfills a greater purpose but also strengthens our bonds with one another and with God.

Practicing gratitude daily helps keep my heart open and my perspective positive, allowing me to recognize the blessings in my life, even on the toughest days. Anchoring myself in God's love provides the strength and foundation I need.

In my journey toward forgiveness, one prayer stood out to me, deeply resonating with my heart. It's the Unity Prayer, which beautifully captures the essence of coming together, not only with others but with God's will. This prayer speaks to me because it aligns with the quiet, transformative work of forgiveness; it's about surrendering our hearts, our minds, and our souls to God's grace. The Unity Prayer comes from the Flame of Love from the Immaculate Heart of Mary, emphasizing the profound connection to divine love and mercy.

The Unity Prayer reminds me that forgiveness is a sacred act that brings wholeness, reconciliation, and peace. It connects me to God and to others, inviting unity, shared purpose, and healing.

The Unity Prayer

"May our feet journey together.
May our hands gather in unity.
May our hearts beat in unison.
May our souls be in harmony.
May our thoughts be as one.
May our ears listen to the silence together.
May our glances profoundly penetrate each other.

May our lips pray together to gain mercy from the Eternal Father."

As I pray these words, I'm reminded that we're all walking this path together, supporting one another through forgiveness and grace. This prayer anchors me in the truth that real peace comes from living in harmony with ourselves, with others, and with God.

It's a daily choice, but every day brings new opportunities to live in peace, to experience the joy of reconciliation, and to share in the love and happiness that God desires for all of us.

The more I forgive, the more I feel my heart open to love, to joy, and to happiness. It's as if forgiveness isn't just about releasing the past but about creating space for all the good that God wants to fill us with peace that surpasses understanding, love that binds us together, and joy that is rooted in the freedom of letting go.

We are meant to live lives of peace and happiness. That is what God desires for us: freedom from the burdens we carry, the chains of unforgiveness that hold us back. So, let's forgive ourselves. Let's forgive others. And let's move forward, one day at a time, knowing that we are walking in the grace and mercy that God has freely given us.

My journey to forgiveness has been filled with waiting, learning, and growing. Through trusting in God's plan, I found peace and joy. True love forgives, and God's timing is perfect. This is the peace I want to share with others, as we all walk this path together. I want to leave you with this: no matter where you are in your life right now, no matter the struggles you may face, choose forgiveness. Choose peace, choose love, choose joy. I believe that God wants us to live in freedom, in happiness, and in the deep, fulfilling connection that comes from true forgiveness.

Gelisa Lewis, LCSW

Founder and CEO of Kami Wellness Counseling and Consulting

https://www.linkedin.com/in/gelisa-lewis-lcsw-cctp-cmip-%F0%9F%92%99%F0%9F%95%8A%EF%B8%8F-898441102/
https://www.facebook.com/share/15RVUFYGv9/?mibextid=wwXIfr

I, Gelisa Lewis am a dedicated mental health therapist from Washington, DC, committed to empowering individuals on their journey to emotional well-being. I earned my bachelor's degree in Social Work from Clark Atlanta University, where I developed a strong foundation in understanding human behavior. I then pursued my master's degree in Social Work at Barry University, gaining hands-on experience in providing compassionate and evidence-based care. Currently, I am the owner of a private practice named in honor of my deceased daughter Kami Wellness Counseling and Consulting. I am licensed to practice in Maryland and Georgia. With a passion for helping others navigate life's challenges, I specialize in anxiety, depression, trauma, crisis intervention, suicide prevention, substance abuse, and relationship issues. As a therapist, my goal is to be the therapist who I needed and wanted while being genuine and nurturing towards others. I want to end the stigma towards mental health.

Tears She'll Never See Me Cry

By Gelisa Lewis, LCSW

Growing Up in Chaos

Growing up as a Black, gay, and poor child meant that every day was a fight for survival. Each of these identities, Black, gay, and poor, carries its own distinct set of challenges. But when combined, they form a perfect storm of struggle, pain, and resilience. The weight of these identities could feel crushing, and yet, each one pushed me to find a way to survive in a world that was constantly trying to diminish me.

My childhood in southeast DC was a stark contrast to the gentrified version you see today. Back then, it wasn't safe to ride your bike outside, but the reality was that I didn't even have the option to do so. I never had the freedom that children are supposed to have. Even as a child, I was treated like a possession, a trophy to be fought over. My parents' constant battles over me shaped the way I understood love and security. My mother became incredibly overprotective, but at the same time, she pushed me to be fiercely independent. But independence, when it's imposed and not nurtured, doesn't create strength; it creates isolation. We needed support, but it was something we never had. I grew up missing out on the simple joys of childhood things like playing sports, going on family trips, or even participating in school events.

From the moment I learned to read, books became my escape. My grandmother would buy me mystery novels, and I would lose myself in the pages, far away from the chaos of my life. I discovered poetry, and it became my voice. I would pour my heart and trauma into words, creating something beautiful from the wreckage of my emotions. The awards I won for my poetry were the only moments when I felt seen, the only times my family acknowledged me. When my work was published in the school paper or celebrated at an awards ceremony, it was the only time I felt like I mattered. But even in those moments, a quiet resentment began to grow. I started to realize that my worth was defined by my accomplishments, not by who I was.

Beyond academics, financial hardship often meant that we lived in unsafe neighborhoods, and that danger became the reason I was kept indoors. I was often told I couldn't attend after-school practices because it was too dangerous outside. I learned to navigate chaos, but the scars I carry are reminders that not all wounds are visible. Over time, I began to take on the role of caretaker, essentially becoming a parent to my mother as much as she was to me. The bond we shared began to fray, and I started to see her less as a parent and more as someone I had to protect.

A Child's Place

Growing up, I could never understand when my mother would tell me to "stay in a child's place." Her words were a constant reminder that my feelings didn't matter. As a child, I was told that my struggles weren't as bad as I thought. I was told to stay silent and accept the world around me. But at the age of 10, everything changed. My little sister was born, and in an instant, I was no longer a child. My days became consumed with caring for her, making bottles, cleaning up, and making sure she was safe. My own childhood slipped away quietly, unnoticed.

As a middle child, I often felt invisible. I was just there to meet the needs of everyone else around me. No one could see the deep resentment that simmered beneath the surface. Before my little sister was born, I had always felt like I was the center of attention in our family, but once she arrived, everything changed. I began to resent her, blaming her for the trauma I had experienced. I was forced to spend time with relatives while my mother dealt with pregnancy complications. And during that time, someone close to the family took advantage of me. I was molested for months, and it started with the seemingly innocent phrase, "Do you want to play a game?"

How could I ever stay in a child's place when my childhood was stolen from me? How could I follow the rules when I was taught that my life didn't matter? The scars from that time aren't just physical; they're emotional, too. My family moved on like nothing ever happened. I was placed in therapy, but my mother's inconsistency meant that the healing I so desperately needed was always just out of reach.

The bigger question that lingered in my mind, though, was whether there was even space for a young, Black, lesbian woman like me to exist in the world I inhabited. I had always known that I was a lesbian, but coming to terms with my identity in a Black community that was deeply influenced by religion and traditional values was an impossible task. Being openly gay in my family and community was seen as a betrayal, something to be ashamed of. Every day, I lived in shame, berated for my sexuality by both my family and my peers. I never understood why it upset my mother so much. My love life had no impact on her, and yet, she treated it as if it did.

It was often said that my sexuality was just a phase, a product of my history of sexual abuse. My family would tell others, "Oh, she hates men," but I didn't hate men. I had spent years processing my anger, but I didn't have room for hate. I was too busy learning to survive in a world that was constantly teaching me to fear it. The fear, though, was never just of the outside world; it was the fear of never being accepted for who I truly was.

Growing Up Too Soon

The weight of shame in my family became too much for my mother to bear, and one day, she simply told me not to come home. It's a memory that still haunts me, the feeling that I had been discarded when I needed her the most. By this time in my life, I had never even had a summer job. Instead, I spent all my summers raising my little sister. My mother would pay me a small amount whenever she felt like it, but I was never allowed the freedom that children should have. I couldn't go outside with friends or enjoy a normal childhood. I didn't have those memories of summers with cousins or visits to grandparents' houses.

The years that followed my junior and senior years of high school were a blur of darkness and fleeting moments of freedom. I finally had the opportunity to live on my own terms, but I had nowhere to go. I wore the same outfit every day for a week, washing it out at a friend's house every night. I tried staying with a family friend, but that just led to more abuse. I searched for a job every day, yet all I could do was pray for a safe space to land.

If it wasn't for the man I now call Dad, I don't know where I would be. The man I thought was my biological father wasn't allowed in my life, and it wasn't until later that we reconnected. My new dad, a close family friend, offered me the safety and love I had so desperately needed. He told me I could come and stay with him and never return to the environment that had nearly broken me. His home became my sanctuary, the place where I could finally breathe and begin to heal.

Having parental guidance, freedom, and genuine love allowed me to thrive. I excelled in high school and went on to attend college, becoming the first and only person in my immediate family to do so. I earned my bachelor's degree from Clark Atlanta University and my master's from Barry University. Despite numerous health challenges, I persevered. As a child, I had always dreamed of becoming a doctor and a gymnast, but I was told those dreams were unattainable. So, I focused on my education. Eventually, I discovered social work, and it felt like the perfect fit. I wanted to be a social worker so I could help other children who had endured the same pain I had. That desire eventually evolved into a passion for becoming a therapist, someone who could help heal others, just like I had needed.

Dark Nights

But the darkness didn't fade once I reached the safety of my new life. PTSD still clung to me, and the weight of my trauma often felt unbearable. I felt like I was constantly fighting an invisible battle, even when I had support. The loneliness, the emptiness, it was always there. I couldn't shake the feeling that life was a series of failures and disappointments, and with each one, the darkness grew deeper. I clung to unhealthy romantic relationships, hoping they would give me the family I had always dreamed of. But those relationships only deepened my wounds. I wasn't aware of my own attachment issues at the time, but looking back, I see how they shaped my choices. Life felt like a constant swing between extremes, either I cared too much, extending myself to the point of exhaustion, or I was so detached that no one could tell if I had any feelings at all.

After completing my master's degree, I decided to start a family on my own using a sperm donor. But life had other plans. At five months pregnant, my water broke. The heartbreak I experienced in that moment shattered me in ways I never thought possible. To give birth to a child I had dreamed of for so long, only to know she would never come home, was a pain that no words could fully express. I chose to have a natural childbirth, part of me wanting to feel the full weight of the experience to know that it was real, even though it hurt more than I could bear. At my lowest point, I wanted to give up. I didn't see how I could keep going, but in that darkness, I discovered my purpose. I needed to heal, and in doing so, I realized that I could help others heal, too. I began my own journey through trauma therapy, and it was the beginning of a new chapter in my life.

Working on Forgiveness

Today, my relationship with my mother remains strained, distant, and complicated. I've forgiven her for sending me into the world without a safety net, but forgiveness doesn't mean forgetting. It doesn't mean that I have to allow the same hurt to keep coming. Forgiveness is about letting go of the pain inside me so that I can heal. It's about cutting ties with the things that hurt me, even if they're unforgettable. I will never forget what was taken from me, the moments when I was silenced, the things I had to endure. But I refuse to let those experiences define me. I've used that pain to fuel my determination to build a better life for myself and others. I've set a new goal: to become an author. And in doing so, I will write about the tears my mother never saw me cry.

JOIN THE MOVEMENT!
#BAUW

Becoming An Unstoppable Woman
With She Rises Studios

She Rises Studios was founded by Hanna Olivas and Adriana Luna Carlos, the mother-daughter duo, in mid-2020 as they saw a need to help empower women worldwide. They are the podcast hosts of the *She Rises Studios Podcast* and Amazon best-selling authors and motivational speakers who travel the world. Hanna and Adriana are the movement creators of #BAUW - Becoming An Unstoppable Woman: The movement has been created to universally impact women of all ages, at whatever stage of life, to overcome insecurities, and adversities, and develop an unstoppable mindset. She Rises Studios educates, celebrates, and empowers women globally.

Looking to Join Us in our Next Anthology or Publish YOUR Own?

She Rises Studios Publishing offers full-service publishing, marketing, book tour, and campaign services. For more information, contact info@sherisesstudios.com

We are always looking for women who want to share their stories and expertise and feature their businesses on our podcasts, in our books, and in our magazines.

SEE WHAT WE DO

OUR PODCAST   **OUR BOOKS**   **OUR SERVICES**

Be featured in the Becoming An Unstoppable Woman magazine, published in 13 countries and sold in all major retailers. Get the visibility you need to LEVEL UP in your business!

Have your own TV show streamed across major platforms like Roku TV, Amazon Fire Stick, Apple TV and more!

Learn to leverage your expertise. Build your online presence and grow your audience with FENIX TV.
https://fenixtv.sherisesstudios.com/

Visit www.SheRisesStudios.com to see how YOU can join the #BAUW movement and help your community to achieve the UNSTOPPABLE mindset.

Have you checked out the *She Rises Studios Podcast?*

Find us on all MAJOR platforms: Spotify, IHeartRadio, Apple Podcasts, Google Podcasts, etc.

Looking to become a sponsor or build a partnership?

Email us at info@sherisesstudios.com

SHE RISES
STUDIOS

www.ingramcontent.com/pod-product-compliance
Lightning Source LLC
Chambersburg PA
CBHW071322120626
46546CB00002B/396